Searching for the Wild Asparagus
23 (or 22) Acres in Newbury, Vermont

I0559261

Essays and Photos by Glenn Reed

ONION
RIVER
PRESS

Burlington, Vermont

Onion River Press
47 Maple Street, Suite 214
Burlington, VT 05401

ISBN: 978-1-957184-50-0

Library of Congress Control Number: 2023924127

Book design by Marian Willmott, www.willmottstudios.com

Acknowledgements

This is a book that I felt I had to do and it is dedicated to my parents, known as "Bill and Bev" to those who loved them. It's also in recognition of the many other people, as well as horses, dogs, cats and other critters, that were a vital and integral part of the fragment of place and time written about in this book. I'm grateful for the wonderful experiences that these 23 acres (or 22) provided to me for 48 years of my life and to the spirit of that place.

Almost all of the photos in this publication were taken by me. They were shot with several different cameras, including a handful with my beloved Pentax MX 35mm (before it was stolen) and others with an old Kodak Instamatic. The pictures were taken over a period of about 45 years and the quality varies. Many are scans of photographs and a large number are digital and there are even some black and white prints (or photos of them) that I developed myself when taking a photography class back in 1983. These are on pages 31, 69 and 81. There are also a few scans of slides for which the photographer is not known. They include the following: pages 25 and 51 are slides of Bill in a sulky; page 82 is a slide of Muffy running in front of Bill who is on a sulky; page 89 is a slide of Bill and friends in winter. The page 101 photo of our house and property from the air is a scan of a small print that was given to my parents (photographer unknown).

Many thanks to Matt for his love, support and advice throughout the long process of completing this publication.

Contents

Foreword—February 2021

I composed the following series of essays back in early 2013 while briefly living in Mount Vernon, Washington. This was during a time of major transitions in my life and about a month before my partner and I determined that it was necessary to move back to Vermont. It was also a bit of a chaotic period for many reasons.

My mood in writing this material was reflective and nostalgic as well as full of sadness for a time and place that I sensed was slowly fading away. I knew what the coming years would bring and that, eventually, I'd have to deal with much loss—including of our family's home of (at the time) about 40 years. Through the process I sought to come to some level of acceptance of the realities, the truths, the mysteries of the human condition that we all face. And recognition of both my own mortality and my place in time and the universe. I'm not sure that I really succeeded but that, of course, is all part of that mystery.

I deliberately focused the essays on the land itself. I could write so much more about our house, the nearby landscape, experiences in the Town of Newbury. There are so many more stories there, and I am writing some of them (short fiction). However, I wanted this collection of essays to focus on those 23 acres and to capture the spirit of that piece of land and my personal relationship to it.

I've revised these essays somewhat in the years since writing them, but tried to stay true to my perspective from that particular time and place as well. In only a few instances have I inserted a few words or a paragraph or two from the present. They hint at the many more changes that have occurred since writing them. And of recent, major losses that have been extremely hard on me and which have altered my ties with that place so much more. I didn't want to write about it from this changed perspective, but remain true to where my head had been while composing the essays when I lived in Washington State's Skagit Valley.

The essays flowed out of me more easily than usual. My writing process is more often one of agonizing over each word, every sentence, grappling with direction, themes, ideas in a brain that too often seems muddled or completely clouded with my all too frequent depression. And, of course, always feeling that my final product is inadequate or worse. Always questioning myself.

I know that a large part of this atypical ease with the writing came from having some physical distance from the subject matter. Over seventeen years of living in the Pacific Northwest and Humboldt County, California, had resulted in my feeling very much at-home there and intimate with the landscape, the climate, the moods and feeling of those special places. Thinking about my old home-- where my parents had (at that time) lived for about 40 years--enabled me to understand what events, what features of that place, what spiritual connection had played key roles in shaping who I had become as a person. I could better connect dots and the resulting picture was easier to discern on those rainy, dark Northwest days and nights of December and January when I sat in a comfy, antique chair and thought back to the many years residing on, or regularly visiting, our old farmhouse and its acreage in Newbury, Vermont.

In writing about specific events or periods of time, I also tried to stay true to where my head was during those years. For instance, my early-to-mid teenage years were fairly typical in terms of my levels of angst, feeling misunderstood, thinking I was a total outsider, not really understanding where my parents or others were at in life or why. Of course as an adult I recognize that they had struggles like everyone else—some of which I wasn't aware of during those years and some that I knew all too well. I acknowledge both the positives and the negatives and how they shaped who I am. I didn't inject my current perspective, and my growth, but tried to remember where I was at, emotionally and spiritually, during those times. I worry that there some sections may be perceived as too critical of my parents, but that's not what I meant to portray at all.

Soon after I had reached what I felt to be a finishing point with these essays we received word that my stepfather, Bill, had been diagnosed with cancer. This, coupled with my mother being in her early 80's and experiencing major health issues, made us decide that we had to return to Vermont and be readily available to assist as-needed. And to have some more quality time with my parents while we still had the chance.

In many ways this was a wrenching decision. The years on the West Coast had helped me explore more about myself than I was able to do back in New England. I felt redefined in many ways and, as already mentioned, I had grown intimately connected to the Pacific Northwest as a place. I also knew that I would feel like a stranger in many respects back where I had spent over thirty years of my early life. I recognized that the land that I had written about so fondly would no longer be the same. In experiencing that now I'm reminded of a line from the film *The Sweet Hereafter*, where a main character speaks of adjusting to a once familiar place following extreme tragedy:

"And everything was new and strange."

This turned out to be both true and not true. In the eight years (when this was written) that we've been back in Vermont, there have been more massive changes in our lives. Most have been the loss of many loved ones. The most significant and traumatic one occurred just last June when my mother passed away at the age of 90. She'd been in a nursing home for over two years at that point and so the character of our Vermont home and property had already changed dramatically. It had become mostly a place that made me sad and feeling I was bearing witness to an ending and a transition of which I wouldn't play much more of a part. At times when I'm there now I feel like a ghost.

I know that this place is one that will be occupied by others who will create something totally different and unique for them. Something that I won't recognize anymore. A place that will become, while I am still alive, one that just fills me with a painful longing, where I'll sense vague movements in my peripheral vision that hint of past times, and that will evoke fleeting feelings that I'll try to grasp onto without success. I'll hear familiar whispers in my brain when I'm going to sleep and thinking of this time and place, but wake to an echo of voices, like the aftermath of a dream. Those 23 acres will then be, in fact, new and strange.

Then it will be time to leave again. And likely not return.

I. Transitory

An aftermath. An epilogue. A denouement. Or none of the above.

Something. A place and a time. Something that was unfamiliar, grew familiar, was ingrained, became so familiar it was painful and joyful all at once. Something that has slowly, imperceptibly, grown unfamiliar again.

Or that I don't want to be made familiar in its new state.

Yes, a place and a time. A time within that time. Arbitrarily pick a point. Say mid-winter, for instance. During a thaw.

Mid-winter thaws are smells and sounds. They drum their fingers with snowmelt dripping from rooftops. They are breathed in with hints of open streams freed from ice and tumbling off the hillsides into hollows and valleys.

Mid-winter thaws roll in heaves through blankets of clouds that envelop all in night's blackness. They whisper of the coming seasons and past moments of listening for echoes of faraway coastlines or trees bending and moaning just near the front porch.

You can stand on the same spots on the back patio or near the barn door where you've always stood. You can stare out and think it could be the previous night or one 30 or 40 years ago. Or any time in-between. As long as it's the night of a winter thaw.

The dark is so thick you can feel it on your face and in your hands. Throughout your whole body. Everything before you is indistinct to your eyes and the field that lies beyond could be the ocean or the sky or the top of a mountain or your childhood dreams or your fears lurking in the closet or unfamiliar, vague shapes when waking up in a strange room or you could be floating in deep space.

Except for the sound and the smell and the sensations on your skin. It's familiar. The refreshing smell of newly melted snow and the faint scent of decaying vegetation and old wood from the barn that offers creaking whispers between the sound from the rise and fall of the wind.

The field's slight undulations are indistinguishable--the line of trees at the far end completely lost in the pitch black against a hint of lighter bulk, where the far-off hills should be. The snow has nothing to reflect and reveals nothing about its depth or its consistency. It huddles into moisture-laden compactness closer to the still-frozen earth, biding its time for when winter, inevitably, returns with a vengeance. You can't tell if the layer of snow has melted down to the point where cut cornstalks poke through or if pools of slushy water have formed in the field's dips and hollows. You can't see where the fence used to stand or where the gray horse is buried or where once stood an apple tree that harbored squirrels that your dog used to chase or the grove of white pines that had once risen beyond the field where, in the past, you used to wander to find a space to be alone.

You can't see these things, but they drift in and out of your consciousness. Images come and go. You're aware of your body, but not. You're 17 years-old and 35 and 25 and 50. You feel that you could be some ghost or a ghost of yourself looking back on yourself staring out into the darkness, the light on the kitchen table spilling out on the back patio, looking back and waiting for yourself to come into view and staring out into the black night, eyes straining to discern the familiar landscape. Imagining a figure standing somewhere out there and looking back.

You remember. At one particular point in time. They've just sold 7 of the 23 acres. The section to the west. In this light, you approximate where the boundary falls, what is no longer officially "the family property." Financial reasons. Winding down in the later years. Two knee and two hip replacements for your mother and a bout with cancer and heart problems with your stepfather. Worse to come. No horses anymore. Fences collapsing. Lives contracting. Upstairs closed off and grab bars in the downstairs bathroom. Items vanishing. Given away or carted off to the landfill. Slowly downsizing. Knowing much more will need to be sold at some point.

Where are the boundaries? Where are the dots and lines in the pitch black? What are 7 of 23 of a continuum of a space in time and place? Where do you point to in the flowing waters of a brook and say I own this piece, this passing of water, these molecules, those atoms? What is yours in the wind that sweeps over the land, picking up particles to whisk them away past the imaginary lines and how do you grasp onto this? Where do you nail in the "No Trespassing!" sign and what is the substance of this language to the steady tear of that wind, the dissolving action of rain, the whittling away of one granule of dirt after another? How can one even begin to own a time, a place, a thought of it all?

At what point does the familiar become unfamiliar? When does "home" become someplace strange? Your own face transform into someone you no longer know? Where does your existence, your space, begin and end? Or does it?

A February thaw. An early July thunderstorm. The corn getting harvested in September. A group of local high school students gathering pumpkins to put in the back of a pick-up. What are you looking at now? What is now?

What do you say at this point that leaks out of your mouth in less than a whisper, is eaten up immediately by the vast silence, that echoes back to ears straining to make out a sound and your memory grasping at some spot in a lit window, kneeling over an uprooted tree, pushing open a barn door, gliding on skates across a sheet of ice?

What more can you say that hasn't already been said or been left unsaid? Is anyone there to even listen? Or just yourself?

II. Remembering

I wonder where to begin in paying homage to a place. A piece of land to which I've been tied for over 40 years. I guess I just dive right into it.

Ironically, with the 23 acres of which I'm thinking, I'm going to start elsewhere and then meander back. That's because, just like my mother, I tend to go on tangents. One of her best friends used to tease her to "Get to the point, Beverly!" Which reminds me of the time when........oh right.

Linear? Too predictable for both of us, I guess.

Mother and I. Preferring the road less traveled. Or saying the hell with it and just wandering completely off-road.

III. Observation

I was never really into science in high school. I'd always gravitated towards the English classes, the arts and the "softer" social sciences. I pretty much perceived art and science to be polar opposites. What possible connection could there be between writing a short story and learning, by rote, the periodic table? The former was all about imagination and creativity. All open to interpretation. The latter? Boring memorization and concrete rules.

Objective, subjective. Fact, fantasy.

At the beginning of my sophomore year in high school we got a new science teacher. One of the first projects she assigned to our biology class in September involved heading off to a spot behind the school's gym in a somewhat overgrown field. This was just where the land began to slope upwards into woods on the side of a hill.

This teacher had each of us pair-up with another student. She next gave every duo some string and four wooden stakes. I think we had to share a few tape measures too. Then, with our "field research" partners we were to select separate, eight-foot by eight-foot (guessing on the exact measurement) plots of ground and designate them with the string and the stakes. Or was it ten feet by ten feet? Doesn't matter.

Of course, any excuse to get out of the classroom was welcomed by us. But when our teacher explained what we were to do, we all thought it was a dumb idea and a waste of time. Most had no clue as to the point of the exercise.

We marked our territories, so to speak, around the fourth week of September when the weather was still warm, the leaves just starting to change color on some of the trees, the grass still green. Once a week, for the rest of that school year, we'd trudge out to our little plots of land and try to detect anything that appeared significantly different. We were practicing to be carefully observant scientists and expected to take meticulous notes that were regularly reviewed by our teacher.

I think that much of what we were supposed to be noting completely escaped most of us.

I don't remember much about our observations beyond the fact that my ten-by-ten-foot square contained a lot of tall grass, maybe some milkweed and goldenrod, and not a whole lot more. The strongest image that comes to mind is of trudging out there on some frigid winter days, when it was a challenge to try to take notes while wearing mittens or gloves on your hands or painfully cold if you took them off to write anything as fast as possible. I remember one such time, when my field research partner and I were stomping in the foot or so of snow that lay on the ground, staring at the seemingly bleak plot before us--then one of us noticing something and pointing it out. We almost got excited. Almost. There were little footprints in the snow. And a trail of what looked like tiny seeds.

So, maybe we did learn something from this exercise after all, though we didn't recognize it at the time. Or maybe some part of me connected this lesson to my having always enjoyed the outdoors, whether being in the woods, beside streams, on hillsides.

I've carried this enjoyment of the careful observation of nature with me through the years since then. It may not have been objective, data recording science, but it's brought me endless joy on backpacking trips as well as when I've just been sitting on a porch chair, watching what's happening in front of me, overhead, and at my feet.

It's meant staring out the kitchen window as goldfinches bicker and chatter over seeds in the feeder, spying a hawk circling above a rocky peak in Washington State's Olympic Mountains and hearing the alarm whistles (in actuality, they're guttural screams) of sentry marmots, and lying on a bit of ground to patiently watch ants as they painstakingly haul bits of food to their nest. I can engage in such activities for many hours and feel absolute peace and contentment.

These moments spent observing are both science in my ongoing fascination with how the world works, and art in that they frequently inspire poetry, music and painting or drawing. Above all else the connectedness felt in these times has no real need to be defined. It allows me to be focused on the present and keep life's stressors at bay. They tie me intimately with place and time.

These moments are also spiritual which, in the end, is both art and science, with no need to distinguish between the two.

IV. Connecting

We moved around a lot when I was growing up. At least up until the summer before my sophomore year in high school when my parents and I ended up in a small, Vermont town on the Connecticut River. My only brother was off to college at that point. Mom and Bill have been in Newbury ever since, though I continued to move frequently for the rest of my life. Both before, then during my college years, in fact, I never lived more than three years in one place. Since then I think my longest stint in one spot has been almost five years.

Wherever we ended up, I would quickly grow ties with the new "place." I think I made friends with the trees before I did with other kids. From an early age I loved to explore woods, splash in brooks, check out the new plant growth poking through the ground in the spring. Much of this love of nature I attribute to my Mom, who frequently took me out for walks in such places from my earliest years and onward.

I have numerous, fond memories of this process of connecting with the spaces around new homes: Jack-in-the-pulpits poking up in April through the brown leaves and mud along a shallow pond in the woods near my maternal grandparents' house in Monson, Massachusetts; the footpath meandering behind our property in Springfield, Vermont where a friend and I kicked fallen leaves in mid-October and eventually emerged from forest onto a former pasture, slowly being reclaimed by those woods; the pine needle-coated forest floor and the bulbous, pink flowers of lady-slippers that appeared in May underneath groves of majestic white pines close to our Palmer, Massachusetts home; the rock-filled, stream that coursed behind our (rented) house in Orford, New Hampshire--its water a coppery-brown tint from the tannic acid of surrounding hemlocks and other conifers.

And then there was the expanse of field that encompassed the bulk of our 23 acres in Newbury, Vermont, the land rolling gently before abruptly ending at the north end. Here a row of trees marked a steep, slippery bank down to a swamp. The field was bordered elsewhere by a huge grove of white pines, rows of old sugar maples and a mix of other trees such as such pitch pines, oak and poplar.

This became my "place" in that period in high school when our biology teacher assigned those tiny plots in back of the school building for us to observe and I wondered at what I should be looking for—not recognizing until years later that I had already been engaging in similar activities throughout my youth. I guess it only qualifies as "play" and not work when it's not assigned by a teacher or dictated to you by some other adult? Maybe it was just my growing phobia towards science and math or just reacting to school assignments when, in fact, I was doing the very same thing exploring the areas on and around our Newbury property throughout the year. Careful observation that was indistinguishable from spiritual immersion.

I was not happy, at first, when we moved to the "farm" in Newbury. We'd just uprooted a little over two years prior, from what my brother and I considered civilization (a small town in western Massachusetts about 18 miles from, Springfield—not exactly the "big city") to a relatively isolated town in the "North Country." The town that we moved to featured a couple of general stores and the smallest high school in the State of New Hampshire— where our stepfather, Bill, was the new principal--and not much else to our ("flatlander") eyes. We really thought we were in the "boonies."

We were not happy about that move, though it was an unavoidable one at the time (another story). Hell, it was 18 miles to the nearest movie theater! Still, I quickly grew attached to the 1840-ish, stone house where we lived next to a brook, nestled between forested hills, and out of sight of our few neighbors. It didn't matter that it was on the relatively heavily travelled east-west Route 25.

The stream that ran behind the house featured a couple of swimming holes, chaotic jumbles of rocks and resting spots under dark hemlocks. Here I could sit and watch water striders skim the surface of placid pools and the occasional frogs that would be startled into disappearing with a "plop" and then glide to the brook's bottom.

The stream produced distinct sounds depending on the weather and the time of year. Or should I say it "spoke?" I grew accustomed to hearing its "voices" on summer nights from my second-story bedroom window or sensing the power of the water on a winter night, when heavy rains from a thaw opened up the ice and transformed the brook into a wild torrent. It roared at those times.

Most of all, the strip of woods along the brook on our property provided a place to escape to and be by myself, away from the demands of my parents to wash the dishes or rake the lawn, away from the occasional arguments, away from the adolescent angst resulting from weekdays at the new school where I was not feeling very accepted, away from boring homework and the growing weight of a recurring (and at that time unrecognized) deep depression that would regularly drag me down throughout my life. It had been a rather chaotic time for the whole family due to our sudden, forced uprooting from a relatively comfortable situation back in Massachusetts, the deaths of both of my maternal grandparents in those couple of years, even our family dog dying from being poisoned by someone.

Place is sanctuary. And bodies of water are particularly ideal for connecting with a place—with nature. They're endlessly changing, mesmerizing with their rhythmic flow, alternately offering quiet contemplation of our origins and the potential joy contained in each moment as well as the realization that nothing is permanent. They can easily get us back in touch with such simple childhood joys as simply rock-hopping in streams, slipping and falling in and getting sneakers and pants soaked.

Unfortunately, due to our having to relocate to this small, New Hampshire town very quickly, my parents ended up being forced to rent at first. The stone house was intended only for a short-term occupancy and the owners even required that we all be gone from it for a full month each summer so that they could vacation there. Their eventual plan was to retire in the house, which meant my parents had to keep searching for a more permanent home.

And so, just after my freshman year in high school, there we were moving again and leaving my beloved stream behind and replacing it with what? Twenty-three acres of what looked like mostly a big, wide-open, dry field. It appeared to be just plain boring to me in comparison. No flowing, energetic stream. No placid pond or sandy lake shore in its place. The only significant water bordering the property was down in a swamp. I couldn't lie in my bed at night and listen to a damned swamp!

That "disappointment" was very short-lived, of course. This seemingly boring "place" turned out to make do. Quite nicely. And my attachment to it took hold in very short order.

The house itself was already a fixer-upper. Initially we thought it had been built in the 1840's, but later determined it was more like the mid-1860's. It was a farmhouse with about 11 rooms, and adjoining, enclosed storerooms, woodshed, two-car garage and a small barn with enough stalls for about six horses. During one period in its history it had served as a nursing home.

Why a house with 23 acres of mostly field? With a half-mile dirt track looping around the bulk of the acreage? Bill was actually into horse racing--harness racing, specifically. He'd first gotten interested in it when attending college in northern Vermont back in the late 1950's. My stepfather could pursue his dream of harness racing and train horses right in back of our house. Or train what first began as a single horse.

About two-thirds of the track's outer edges were bordered by trees, including those where the land sloped down to the swamp. White pines, pitch pines and oaks, lots of poplars, one prominent red pine, some stately old sugar maples on the south and east sides. The rest went by open pasture and our back yard. On the inside of the track was the expansive field. And a few groves of trees. There was one white pine, in particular, that stood out, anchoring the southeast corner next to a very small excavation. All by itself. It was not very tall when we first moved there.

The field was typically used by a nearby farmer. Some years he planted corn there, and others he used it for haying. In the latter case, he'd later worked out a deal so that Bill would get the bales from the first cutting, and the farmer would take the second crop. Or was it the reverse? Doesn't matter.

That first cutting would typical occur in mid-to-late June and I never looked forward to it. Not that I minded the hard work, but it always seemed that the haying would happen during a very hot and humid spell. This meant profuse sweating, skin coated with dust and bits of the hay, and lots of itching and countless, tiny scratches.

We'd usually get about 800 bales from each cutting. Bill would try and get neighborhood kids, or some from the high school, to help out too, but I'd always end up being one of those picking up bales and heaving them on the back of the pick-up rather than stacking them. Then I'd have to toss them from the pick-up to the hay loft in the top of our small barn while our helpers stacked them inside. We had no conveyor for that task. Of course, as the pile in the back of the pick-up got lower from unloading, it meant that I had to toss the bales ever higher. Tiring work.

Oh well. It was just once a summer.

The year that we moved to Newbury, the neighboring farmer had planted most of the inner field with corn. This area comprised about two-thirds or so of its acreage. The rest, to the west, had been recently planted with rows of white pines by either the previous owner or the same, neighboring farmer, I'm guessing, who eyed their potential timber value a few decades down the line. There were probably four or five rows of these saplings that stretched north to south and I'd guess they totaled 75-100 saplings. Probably more.

We'd moved into the farmhouse around early-July. By that time, the corn had already reached a bit beyond my height. Maybe six feet tall. This was a positive, in my mind. Walking along the half-mile track I could quickly reach a point where no one could see me from the house. Though still within earshot of a loud yell, I could fake otherwise and claim "I couldn't hear you," if I'd been summoned for something and didn't show up in short order. Of course if I disappeared for these "connecting with the land" times I could still be in trouble if there were some chores to be done.

Some asides here. I'm trying to write this as I remember my perspective as the confused and often tortured (in my own head, but typical) young teenager that I was at the time. I had been a bit targeted/picked-on from the 5th grade through my first years of high school and my self-esteem had been pretty decimated. Not that this isn't the experience of so many (most?) teenagers.

I'd also been extremely close to my maternal grandparents, particularly as we (Mom, my brother and myself) lived with them for close to three years after my parents divorced. By the time we had moved to the farm, I only visited with my distant, biological father once a year and then, mid-way through high school, years began to pass between visits. Somehow he always managed to make me feel worse about myself. I acknowledge that it may not all have been with deliberate ill-intent on his part and I didn't recognize the role of our overall family dynamics. Eventually, my contact with him diminished to the point of nothing. To me this felt necessary for my emotional self-preservation. Anyway, losing my maternal grand-parents at a young age was devastating to me and also adversely affected the whole family in many different ways.

The other side of the track quickly became my new refuge from my struggles, if only for a short time. At least in my head. Of course, once Bill had acquired and started to train his first horses, it would not be an escape when he was driving them around the track. I'd have to get out of the way and be careful not to spook the horse when I heard that "clop, clop, clop" getting closer. Sometimes I'd scamper down an old path squeezed between the white pine grove and the swamp. At the bottom I'd barely skirt past the muck at one point while holding on to the branches of some young hemlocks to stay balanced, then negotiate a small break in the wire fence that separated our property from the railroad tracks running parallel to the west of it. Beyond, after walking about a mile or so down those tracks and past a more open area of swamp, was a whole other world to explore. It's where I could access the prominent, wooded ridge that stretched north to south.

Still, "the other side of the track" usually sufficed as a refuge from any stressful family dynamics or a "bad day at school" that added to my frequent anxiety, increasingly intense abdominal cramps, and feelings of helplessness. And the depression that so often engulfed me.

I will leave much unspoken here. The histories, the family issues, all of the variables that interact in making us who we turn out to be in life. Recognizing how those same forces shaped my parents and others. Valuing the positives. Understanding the negatives. I can acknowledge them. I can try to extricate myself from the drag of anything negative. I can embrace all of the good that is integral to other family members and to me. The divorce. Living with my grandparents. Mother remarrying. My stepfather, Bill, getting thrust into a family with two, older children. The effect of my maternal grandparents' deaths when I was just entering my early teens. Our frequent moves. Mom's drinking mixed with Bill's often short temper. My feeling that I was marginalized for so many of my elementary and high school years.

The free-floating tension and the murky clouds of depression descended with more regularity throughout my teens. In school, with friends and family, I was not liking myself. Not comfortable in my own skin. Friends would often comment on my moodiness. I heard the word "introvert." Some days no matter what I did, it seemed wrong. Or so it seemed to me at the time. In response I'd seek the relief of "place" more and more. Those hours immersed in nature saved me. They still do. On a stream by myself or walking through a field or exploring the woods I was connected. And the depression would lift like a morning fog before the rising sun (sorry for the tired analogy).

Reading this narrative now I hope it doesn't sound angry. It's not meant to be at all. Is it a need for processing my past experiences? Maybe. I guess that we spend our entire lives coming to terms with our own histories and how they shaped us. I'm trying to remember what it was like to be in my own head in a time long ago. I know I see things quite differently now though, of course, so many of the patterns set in my youth remain with me. For better or worse. I hope I have a better perspective, especially in having lived some of what my parents and others experienced, while recognizing that we all struggle with the human condition.

And what is most often remembered, for me now, are positives and what has remained consistent. That includes my always seeking those special places outdoors. Still connecting spiritually to place. And the good things about my parents, so many others, and of our Newbury house and those 23 acres.

V. Futility

I was just 15 at the time. It was a very hot, sticky day in late July, after a sweltering week. Haze had enveloped the ridge beyond our property to the west and north. It completely washed out the view of Black Mountain, Sugarloaf, and the 4,802-foot Mt. Moosilauke in New Hampshire's White Mountains to the east. They were usually visible from our field on sunny days when the air was less oppressive and murky.

I'm not sure of the details, but I think Mom and I had been off somewhere for part of the day. When we returned home, Bill said something about my needing to help him out with some work in the field. Within five minutes we were headed back there in his big, green Ford pick-up as a few rumbles sounded from the west, threatening of the thundershower we wished for to break the humidity.

As we rounded the barn, I was saddened to see that all of the rows of three-foot high white pine saplings had been torn out of the ground—uprooted and left lying on the disturbed earth. It looked like battlefield carnage to me.

"We need to pick them all up and take them to the other side of the track and throw them over the side," Bill said. Or something like that because, of course, I don't remember exactly. He didn't tell me why the trees had been dug up. I think that I later learned, at some point, that this section was going to be used for haying and/or planted with corn in future years. This was a more productive use of the space for the short-term (meaning decades since it would take most of our lifetime for those saplings to grow to a "harvestable" point).

All I saw at that time seemed like waste and doomed trees. Something in me had always hated to see trees chopped down or uprooted like that. Clear-cuts made me sick inside. And still do. I felt as if I could almost sense the trees' pain.

It took us a little over an hour for this chore. Afterwards, I felt I needed to do something to mitigate my sadness and try to save some of these fledgling white pines. But I didn't want to be seen because I thought Bill would view it as a pointless waste of time which, in fact, it was.

My mother was too "sentimental." My stepfather was more "practical." So often they seemed out-of-balance with each other and so much effort was put into trying to achieve some equilibrium. I remain overly sensitive and sentimental but, hopefully, have managed to recognize the "practicality" in any situation and strive for a functional balance. Left brain, right brain, yin and yang, science and art. However, it often seems that when I choose what seems to be the more practical course, things end up going off-the-rails. Or vice-versa.

Or I go on these tangents. Just like Mom.

Anyway, on that early summer evening I crept to the barn after dinner, grabbed a shovel, and went to the west side of the track, where I hoped I could make my way around the corner without being seen by my parents from our house. At that point it was less than an hour before sunset. I had no idea how many trees I could try to replant in the time before it grew dark, nor did I have a clue if they would survive or if I could try saving any of them the next day. Still, I felt that if I could give at least eight or ten of them another opportunity to grow on the outside edge of the track, it would make me feel better.

I never realized how much work it is to dig a hole. At least one deep enough to plant a small tree. Especially in ground covered with weeds, the occasional aspiring bush, and crisscrossed underneath with a network of roots from the nearby trees. Not to mention the frequent large rocks. Thank you, glaciers.

It seemed that with every other plunge of the shovel into the ground, it jammed against something. After less than an hour, as the flat, gray light of the cloudy sky rapidly faded in that sweltering dusk, I was soaked in sweat and tired of swatting at the endless hordes of deer flies that circled my head and which bit with relish. It almost felt as if they were mocking my efforts. And no matter how deeply I dug, it seemed that the roots of the few small trees that I tried to replant would not easily fit in the holes. My painstaking effort to save a few of the white pine saplings all seemed to be futile.

After having attempted to plant about six or seven trees, the light was almost gone and I had to head back to the house. All the time I had wondered if I could be seen from our kitchen's picture window that offered a panoramic view of our field and the foothills behind. Probably not.

I never did find out. Neither Bill nor Mom asked where I'd been. After all, it wasn't unusual for me to wander off around the track or into the woods on the other side.

Nor did a single one of those white pines survive. I checked on them the next day and saw their needles quickly turning brown. After just a few days it was clear that they were all dead.

Why does this incident resonate with me now, over forty years later? An example of the futility I've felt throughout my life, no matter how hard I tried? Futility in dealing with family issues, finding jobs, maintaining relationships, dealing with a feeling of alienation from society, the promises of breaks in life that fell through? Even the futility of the seemingly endless rejections for my writing, carefully filed away in a bulging folder as another reminder of my failings?

What was wrong with me, I wondered at that time when I was in my mid-teens? Typical adolescent angst, I guess, though I'd felt that I was one of only a handful in its throes of misery.

Or maybe I'm reading too much into it. Maybe I just didn't like to see something die if there was any way that I could help prevent it.

Days after the uprooting of the white pines, I was still escaping to the far side of the field or beyond. I'd been saddened by the death of those white pine saplings, but managed to find peace in what remained in the area where I'd tried to give them another chance. I'd focused on the patches of red-capped British soldiers and the reindeer lichen thriving on the well-drained, sandier soils beneath the full-grown white pines. I'd listened to the chattered scolding of squirrels and "caw-caws" of the crow that landed at the top of a prominent, red pine at the other end of the track. I'd poked around the overturned and rotting rowboat, wondering why on Earth there was a rowboat on the edge of our field. I'd looked through the gutted, rusted 1940's auto and other debris that had been dumped over the bank by some previous residents of our house and that were slowly decaying and migrating down towards the swamp.

Still, decades later that sense of futility remains inside of me. And large-scale clear-cuts, such as those I regularly saw while living back in Washington State, still upset me when I see them (knowing now, of course, that massive clear-cuts are NOT a wise forestry practice). But I remain determined to grab a shovel and try to replant something. To save something. After all, as they say, scratch beneath the surface of any cynical person and you find a constant glimmer of optimism.

I'm still trying to find that line between persistence and insanity, hope and utter despair. In the end I guess I'd rather be spiritually connected to the earth around me rather than indifferent to it. I'd rather not place human "civilization" on a pedestal that is, supposedly, God-ordained, according to far too many people. I'd rather be crazy than heartless. Tilting at windmills.

Crazy it is, then. Or destined to be like Sisyphus, futility be damned.

VI. Framing

What is place?

What is it that makes a place familiar? What makes it both familiar and unfamiliar? What makes it slowly spread roots and ensnare your soul? When does that happen?

Does it ever let go? What happens to you if it does?

What is it about standing in one spot, closing your eyes, and feeling the time flow by as if you're standing in a stream? Sometimes you sense it as actual liquid. Just like water. What makes it both the place where you stood with your eyes closed thirty years prior or twenty years before and know that you remember all moments as if you are present in them all at once? And feel yourself there five or ten years in the future?

In eight-by-eight foot, squared plots of land, the seed for a bush will take root and grow within a year. The brown, dead grass and other plants flattened under winter's heavy snows will eventually emerge with new green shoots that will thicken and then fill with asters and goldenrod by late summer.

In twenty-three acres of field and a border of woods much will take root and grow as well, rise towards the sky, be cut, be replaced, grow again. When you close and open your eyes repeatedly as you stare out at the twenty-three acres, it's like a rapid slide show. Or time lapse photography. Or an old 8mm film. Flickering. But it's overlapping and moving away and other scenes move in. Fluid. In the same place, but not. You move repeatedly and you always stand still. You extend in all directions.

Twenty-three acres can be a lesson in succession. In peace and stability, tragedy and loss, recovery and renewal. It can be a sheltering grove of dozens and dozens of towering white pines that seem to anchor the field to the foothills beyond. That grove becomes a place to go and meditate, sit cross-legged in the soft pine needles, feel sheltered from the wide exposure of the field. They can hide details of the ridge due to their proximity and foliage, details like the bowl cut into the open bedrock by glaciers thousands of years prior, thus encouraging you to venture down the footpath that skirts the swamp, leads through a gap in the tangled wire fence line, invites exploration down the railroad track and into the woods well beyond your property. The 23 acres can whisper into your soul to go forth, but never leave at the same time.

The stateliness of the white pines dominated the view from the picture window of our Newbury home during our first years there. In the summer, the rows of corn seemed to converge towards them. When the field was hayed, the bales and then the newly cut field created a symmetry that they helped balance. The smaller poplars, red maples and oaks paid homage along the sections of track that led up to the white pines. Those trees were majestic.

Then one day, over half of them were gone. The perspective was altered.

The resulting view reminded me of an open mouth with every other tooth missing. Features of the foothills were then partly visible through the gaps. It was no longer a real grove. Or intimate. It felt violated and vulnerable. No longer nature, but a resource.

Practical, are resources. You can't eat sentiment. The trees brought my parents some needed cash. But when in your teens, you can't balance these realities in your head.

A new perspective then grows. Balances things out again. Accentuates a different beauty. You grow older. You see the endless transformations.

Over the summer following this cutting, undergrowth quickly spread around the remaining white pines. Saplings took advantage of the more open canopy and increased sunlight pouring through it. Little white pines took root. Raspberry bushes. Poplars. More deer were spotted browsing at dusk at the edge of field near the remaining trees.

Succession. Before my eyes. Just no longer the spot for quiet meditation in the shade on a hot summer afternoon. A change of perspective. In the same place, but not. Another lesson.

A few years later, on a visit home from college, I found them all gone. Totally disappeared. What felt like a gaping hole in the northwest corner of the field. An opening that completely revealed the bowl shape in the hillside and its exposed bedrock. Now able to see the hawk occasionally circling over its domain there. No longer an anchor to the 23 acres, but like an outlet for the land to funnel through, slowly eroding down into the swamp that arcs in the floodplain of the nearby Connecticut River. Imagining geologic succession: the glaciers scouring and depositing, retreating and melting, the lake growing and then shrinking, slowly disappearing, the terracing, the river winding and sections cut off into oxbow ponds and swamps and then filling in over the years to eventually become solid ground.

But, the trees.

Trees are essential to place and to connection. Their distinctive barks, their textures, their leaves, the shape of their canopy, their preference for the make-up of the earth in which to grow, their attraction for other plants, animals, insects, what creatures nest in them, what eats them. Their place in the web of life.

The bulk of the 23 acres can be framed by the picture window. And the trees add balance, substance, character, shading, color.

When some are gone, others will eventually replace them. The scene will always continue to trend in one direction. Towards a balance.

VII. Snapshots

My beloved Pentax MX 35mm camera. I had it for about 35 years before it was stolen (No! Digital is not quite...the same).

Click.

The butternut lies roughly fifteen feet past the back patio. Rough, creviced bark, ideal for the squirrels nesting in a hole near a crook of the tree. Green and sticky husks protect the butternuts that accumulate on the ground. Beyond, the gnarly crabapple with several rotting branches. To the right, on the track's first bend, the lone white pine rising with its wide girth and about twenty feet tall right where the earth was gouged out at some time years ago. Someone digging out a few truckloads of the rich soil? The lone red pine at the second bend in the track to the north, poking into the sky twice as far and the full-grown white pine near it seeming to be entangled in cumulus clouds. The row of poplars that applaud in breezes with their small, fan-like leaves. The thick grove of tall white pines in the far, northwest corner and the cluster of eight-foot high white pines that emulate them and are taking hold on the opposite side of the track, bordering the corn field. The stalks of corn, riding the ripples of the field, basking in the hazy sun. The fence around the barn weathered, broken in spots. The garden hose snaking away from the spigot on the side of the house rushing water to the old bathtub, which trickles that water over its side as it runs in-place with clawed feet.

Click.

The longest branch from the butternut has fallen, the victim of a late summer thunderstorm and the tree's weakness from rot. Another branch appears to be in rough shape. Downy woodpecker taps loudly for a mate, scampering in bursts up its side, an urgency spoken in the red patch on its head. The crabapple tree. Gone. Just a stump remaining. Grasses growing in the field and awaiting dry weather for the first cutting for hay. Jittery sky, saturated with southern and Atlantic-fed moisture, but not sure when to let loose. White pine at the track's first bend. Now about twenty-five feet high. Poplar grove exuberant with open sky and unobstructed sun rising in the northeast corner near the lone, white pine and red pine. More than half of the white pine grove missing from the northwest corner. The opposite grove in adolescence, its trees now standing uniform in height at about 10 to 12 feet. Abstract iron-oxide deposition patterns spreading on the side of the bathtub near the barn. New cross-sections in the fence, wood smooth and bright in contrast to the weathered posts. Two horses stomping and snorting in the paddock adjoining two sides of the barn as a steady trot taps a cadence on the opposite side of the track. The sulky and its seated figure being led by a horse down the straight-away. Passing by and then disappearing behind the young, white pines.

Trot, trot, trot....

Click.

A clear view across the yard now, to the field. Four- foot round, rotting stump where the butternut tree once rose and spread its limbs. A new fence put in to make a bit of pasture bordering the house side of the track. Two horses there placidly nibbling at grass, red clover and alfalfa. They've discovered the remaining apple trees in the other corner of the back yard, where the mottled fruit thumps to the ground. The horses anxiously munch on them, getting intoxicated with the summer afternoon. Corn planted again on the main field. Small plot of vegetable garden in one of its corners, with green beans racing tomatoes, squash, cucumbers and broccoli to first picking. Field bindweed with their white flowers and clusters of blue vetch with their rows of fish-scaly leaves crowding the new fence posts. Two figures amble along, barely distinct, in the northwest corner. Mom and a visiting friend walking around the track.

Click.

No white pines in the northwest corner of the 23 acres. Visible are the serpentine curves of the ridge beyond and the bowl-shaped indentation. Easy to follow are the dips and arcs of a hawk as it scans the distant terrain for a meal. Row of hemlocks lining the path down to the swamp and their tops now slightly visible from the house. The adolescent grove on the inside of the track now in young adulthood. The bulk of the poplars in the northeast corner have been cut. Staghorn sumacs stand prominent in bushy tangles. Several figures head around the first bend of the track with the white pine on their left. My brother. Two young girls by his side, getting fidgety, decide to run ahead. My nieces.

"See the tree how big it's grown." You and your brother once laughed at the sappy song with that lyric. Now you experience it. You still laugh, but at a different joke.

Click.

Poplars have risen in the northwest corner, skirted by the thorny chaos of raspberry bushes. Clumps of goldenrod and black-eyed Susans splash bits of color through the surrounding grasses and oak or white pine saplings struggling to take hold. The bulk of the hemlocks have disappeared and the grove of aspiring white pines never reached full adulthood. The pitch pines on the drier, west side of the track are mostly gone and the exposed under-growth bakes in the hot, summer sun. The fencing around the barn has disappeared, as has the old bathtub. The former paddock now just a continuation of the back lawn. The fence directly behind the house and on the inside of the track is weathered, broken, rotting, with some posts hidden under tangled blackberry bushes. The contents of a large vegetable garden rapidly ripen in neat rows between the yard and the track. A figure bends down to pull off green beans and plop them in a bucket. Mom. The track, itself, is more of a path overgrown with rabbit's foot clover, tufts of grass, and plantain. Two-thirds of the main part of the big field is planted with rows of sunflowers. Their long petals are just starting to turn yellow and they bend their heavy heads to the east where the sun peeks over the summit of Mt. Moosilauke every morning. Another third of the field is corn, with one small section tangled with the big leaves and round, greenish globes of rapidly bulking-up pumpkins.

Click.

VIII. Space

What is space?

Our eight-by-eight-foot plot in high school. We always took notes on what we saw, what was in front of us, what was grounded.

We never thought much about what was below, though the evidence that something was below would become more and more apparent. It would grow. From that ground. From that soil. From underneath. It would occupy more of that space. Above the ground. Reach beyond it to the sky. The seemingly boundless space.

But what about below that unseen and porous, rich, malleable soil? Sand or gravel? From glacial days? And beneath that......solid rock? From volcanic activity? Granite maybe? Or phyllite or schist? Slowly eaten way by the seepage of water over millions of years? Chemical processes? Pressure? A light rainfall? Shifting in response to gargantuan, but unseen tectonic activity? Microscopic changes? At the molecular level or smaller than that?

And above that space. Air. Precipitation falling down. Winds bringing things in and taking things out. Pollen from other trees, bushes, flowers. Birds and bats dropping their excrement, some of which contains seeds, nourished by the rains, taking hold in the ground, sprouting, eaten by other birds or mice that burrow. Back to earth. Processed and enriched by countless earthworms.

Under the ground. Of that space. But is it truly a defined space? Are the years really linear?

We're so obsessed with boundaries. In the end, are there really any?

IX. Hidden

Much is hidden on those 23 acres.

So much is hidden that you may never find or that might surprise or shock you if you did. So much may be hidden by you, as well. Only you, or you and a family member or two may know about something hidden. Maybe deliberately buried. And if one or two others know, when they are gone it will just be you again. Knowing what is hidden. Then when you're gone......

Maybe you, yourself, don't really know some of the things you've hidden there. Or if so, where they are.

Our farmhouse was built around 1840 or so. At least that's what my parents determined when we first moved in and what we told people for the next 30-plus years. Then my parents obtained information indicating that it was probably constructed in the early to mid-1860's.

This was very disappointing. Older was always better. More impressive to others. Especially some friends and family who lived and may have grown up in modern cul-de-sac or suburban neighborhoods where "old" was anything before the 1950's or 1960's or so.

Still, our house qualified as fairly old. Relatively speaking.

Some time when I was around ten years old, I became obsessed with digging for old bottles. I'd seen collections of them at my best friend's house back in Palmer, Massachusetts, and was completely fascinated by them. I loved the colors, designs and interesting embossing on many of them. And the lids that needed corks. Made long before screw-on tops. And the seams that only went part of the way up the necks or the lips of the older bottles.

I soon learned all I could about the hobby. I bought a book on bottle digging and one June day set out with my mother to a site we'd heard about from my maternal grandfather while on a summer trip to my grandparents' retirement home on Cape Cod. Our haul ended up filling a wicker basket and featured such finds as bottles embossed with "The Great Atlantic and Pacific Tea Company" and "Sawyer's Crystal Bluing."

I had to look up exactly what "bluing" entailed, but the latter bottle was, in fact, a beautiful, light blue color.

So, moving to the old farmhouse got me excited at the prospect of finding an old dump site on our property and unearthing dozens and dozens of antique bottles. That first month there, in fact, one of my very first excursions was to follow the track out to where it ran parallel to the swamp and then I cut through the thick undergrowth on the long slope down to where our property ended at the swamp's edge.

Summer, unfortunately, is not the best time to look for dump sites or to dig for bottles, including on our 23 acres. The circling and biting deer flies were relentless in June, July and August, while the mosquitoes delighted in the murky, stagnant pools of the swamp and were drawn, for easy meals, to mammals that ventured and lingered nearby. There were also patches of poison ivy and poison oak lurking in the undergrowth, not to mention that the latter was so dense that it made negotiating the woods a chore—particularly on a steep, bank that was slippery with deep and decaying leaf litter, exposed tree roots and saplings. Not to mention debris from people—from the recent and more distant past.

I did manage to locate a few areas that had clearly served as major dump sites, but due to the thick vegetation, it was difficult to discern their age or if they had already been dug up by others. These were all close to the giant white pine and lone red pine in the northeast corner of the property. All of the spots were covered with some completely whole bottles, many more that were broken, and plenty of glass shards. There were also cans of various shapes in different stages of rusting/decaying, bits and pieces of farm or automobile equipment, shattered light bulbs, springs and screws, damaged sap or water buckets and many other items. There were plenty of beer and soda bottles but most of those in clear view were of the screw-top variety. Not old. Disappointing. There was also a preponderance of Pepsi bottles in one area. Nothing very valuable on the surface that I could see. Little indicated the age of the dump site to be much more than three or four decades at the most.

I carefully looked in the chaos of garbage, leaves, tree roots and ferns for evidence that it had been dumped in for a much longer time--say 80 to 100 years or so. Such signs as a broken bottle top that was made for a cork and not a twist-on or pop-off cap. Or a bottle neck with a seam that didn't go all the way to the top. Any broken piece of an old bottle might indicate that more could lie underneath.

It was also entirely possible that the newer human debris on the surface might be totally covering much older stuff. That the dump had been used for a longer period than just years or a few decades and was layered, with the older bottles and other items deep underneath. Occasionally I would just pick a spot and dig down in hopes of finding something older. All too many times I would quickly reach a layer of just soil, with no more human trash beneath it. Then I would move on to another spot to dig.

That first time that I investigated this part of our property, my heart was beating with excitement that I'd discover a mother lode of antique bottles. I wished there would be so many that it would take all summer to dig through the area and I'd end up with basket upon basket to lug back to the house for careful cleaning and eventual display or sale. I'd have shelves and windowsills full of antique bottles—just like the pictures in my first bottle book!

Of course, it wasn't to be.

I did find plenty of evidence that the site dated back to the late 1800's, but I also found indications that someone had beaten me to the punch here. This wasn't that surprising, as bottle digging had been a popular hobby during the 1970's, but it was still a big let-down. I think--after many trips that summer to this part of our property, much sweating, endless digging through the soil with a metal rake, shovel and trowel--that I probably found about ten worthwhile bottles.

Nevertheless, every few years after that, I'd be motivated to head back with my tools and dig around. I'd scramble up and down the bank, poke around at the edge of the swamp, follow the slope to areas behind a neighbors' property. The next house to the east of ours was much older, as was the one past that. Maybe, just maybe, I'd missed the ideal spot or would locate one that no one else had found yet. Hope springs eternal for treasure-hunters, I suppose. Or was this as futile an exercise as my attempt to replant those white pines?

About thirty years after we moved to this property, and before I permanently (for now) moved back from the West Coast, I did find one small area with a few old bottles that had been overlooked. Not any mother lode, but certainly the eight or ten I unearthed were exciting enough. Other pickers had missed them somehow. At least, I thought, there was a tiny reward for this persistence.

The winter of 2011-2012 turned out to be one of the mildest and most open ever in Vermont. High temperature records were shattered right and left in March and what little snow that had accumulated, even in the higher elevations, soon disappeared. The ground thawed in places where it didn't normally do so until April and May. At least that had been the norm with our old climate.

Conditions were unique then, with the ground rapidly becoming unfrozen, softening, the undergrowth not yet sprouting, the detritus from the previous fall matted out, and the landscape bared for close examination. I'd never had such a chance to peruse the dump site that early in the spring, so one weekend when visiting my parents, I eagerly searched for tools in the garage and then headed out along the track.

What my parents hadn't mentioned to me was that some people had stopped by the previous autumn and asked if they could check the property for dump sites and to dig for old bottles. I quickly discovered that those people had meant business. I found, at the site, a huge excavation gouged into the bank, exposed tree roots jutting out and hanging in the air, whole discarded bottles and debris trailing down the slope to the swamp's edge. They'd dug far deeper than I ever had done before and I worried that they had, in fact, been motivated by discovering a rich vein of old bottles. I cursed myself for not being persistent enough in the past. How dare they?

Several hours later I had a basket filled with about fifteen bottles. Only a handful were unique or valuable finds, but the rest were, at least, from the period of 1880 to 1910 and I was satisfied with the haul. I tried not to obsess about any of the choice specimens that the couple might have unearthed. Many of the ones they'd tossed aside as not worthwhile were ones that I would eagerly have saved in my youth. Maybe they had been worth more at some time, but apparently not now. But I still liked the way that they looked.

All of those decades, when I was resigned but disappointed that there was nothing left to be found on our property, those bottles were lying there in-wait. I have an idea that there may be more that I'll never find.

Probably some day in the distant future, someone will be digging up what we left on that property as well. They'll make guesses about us and our lives there. The clues will be scattered. Disconnected. Vague. Mixed together with others who lived here or nearby. Most will remain a mystery.

And many of the things that we, ourselves, buried will also stay hidden.

X. Running

Running.

I'm running in front of a horse. Holding the reins. Trying to keep a steady rhythm. Hearing the sound of the hoofs landing on the packed dirt. The horse's first time hobbled and pulling the sulky and my stepfather's weighty bulk.

I'm not feeling terribly secure. I'm not a horse trainer.

Eventually, the horse's pace is too much for me. Four legs create that kind of advantage. I let go and the two-- Bill, and the somewhat confused horse--continue around the bend. I keep on running. When I get to the side of the track where it's connected to the dirt road that passes by our house, I head out in that direction so I can do a longer run of my own. At my own pace.

Another time. Visiting the farm and lying down in my old bedroom for a nap. Many years later. Different horses.

The bang of pots. The slight, but annoying, whirring sound of a cheap alarm clock. Other indications of my mother puttering around in the kitchen.

The hoof beats fading. Receding into the distance. Almost imperceptible. Gone. Then dozing. Dreaming.

A race.

I'm desperately looking for my running shoes. They aren't anywhere to be found. Everyone else has taken off running.

Next. The trail starts in a park. I'm running barefoot. I'm in the lead. Then I'm in an office building and looking for signs with directions of where the race course goes, but I don't see any. I hear footsteps coming up behind me.

Then eyes fluttering open. Disoriented. A dresser in my sight. A nightstand.

I'm trying to awaken, latch onto consciousness, the present. Mother is standing next to the bed. She's saying something. Urgency in her tone. Something about....

No. A sad story for another time.

It was a track, after all. For horses. That's a major reason the 23 acres attracted my stepfather. Along with the barn. Bill was into horse racing.

I don't know how much Mom knew Bill was into horse racing when they got married. But Mom learned more about it within the next few years when Bill would take off once in a while with friends to go to the races. Green Mountain Raceway south of Bennington, Vermont. Or Hinsdale, in New Hampshire. Mostly. The occasional town or county fairgrounds. I can't remember when Mom started to go as well. I suppose I could ask, but then this wouldn't be writing solely from my memories.

The farm was the opportunity to live this dream for Bill. So after moving there he acquired his first horse and some sulkies and other needed racing equipment with which I'm not familiar. Things like hobbles and such. Well, I guess I do know now what those are for.

The horses came and went over the years. Standardbreds. Didn't know that term before either. Chestnut brown, with dark manes. Beautiful animals with pleasant dispositions.

There were regular race winners, many more with potential, the foals that pranced in the paddock, some that were mischievous and others that were wary of people. There was the old gray mare (not a race horse), which had nothing but (probably deserved) contempt for humans and wouldn't let you touch her. We just called her "Gray Horse." There was the darker maned one who, I swear, had an impish glint in his eyes. He'd wait for us to turn our backs so he could take a playful nip out of butts or arms, then pull his head back up when you turned around and give that "who me?" expression. It was never a hard bite. Just enough to get your attention.

Don't tell me that horses don't have personalities. Or a sense of humor.

The horses would trot and pace the property into a kinetic vision with multiple laps around the track, trotting out a steady cadence to the cold fronts and fall foliage and fiddleheads unfurling in the spring. Okay—we didn't have any fiddleheads on the property. How about catkins opening up on the poplars? The horses would measure out the days in a rhythm of munching grain, gallops in the paddock, kicking the stall doors and nickering in demand for their nightly hay.

Can you ride them? No. Do you help train them? No. The typical questions from friends, family and others. It didn't count that I led a few for short distances by running in front of them.

But I always liked to watch them. I'd fill their grain bins. I liked to go stroke their necks and give them the occasional carrot. I sketched their shapes in pencil and took endless photos of them in color and black and white. Some were framed and hang in our chilly mudroom and near the piano in the living room. I don't remember which horses anymore. Their old racing pictures curl up and turn yellow in the barn, where they hold victorious heads up to spider webs and ghosts. I look at them now as the stalls around me sit empty and still.

I see the smiling faces of people with those horses in those photos, captured in that moment of winning. Many or even most of those people are gone now as well.

I turn, almost expecting to feel a nip at my sleeve. I listen, but there is no nickering in anticipation of nightly hay. I stare out the propped-open barn door at the field stretching off to the trees and the ridge beyond.

XI. Misstep

This other time. A painful story to recall.

The bang of pots. The slight, but annoying, whirring sound of a cheap alarm clock. Other indications of my mother puttering around in the kitchen.

So, the pieces.

Mother. Perhaps preparing lunch.

A prize horse; a part of the dream. A regular winner. The one horse of a lifetime. Bill excited.

A weekend visit for me. A July day lazing away in haze, iced tea and rotating fans. Feeling tired. Taking an afternoon nap.

Dreams of mid-summer and life high at this apex. Breathing in the air with relish, strong and determined, at full speed with adrenalin rushing and chasing the sky and everything redolent of green and ripeness and the road stretching to the horizon.

Lightning out of the gate, the enthusiastic cheers and encouragement from the crowded stands, the other horses jockeying to each side, the drivers hard on the reins and the slight sting of the whip. Slowly, but surely, inching ahead. Then doing so more rapidly and then that last effort, the full push for the finish. Time slowing down then. To a crawl. Frozen.

The door thrust open. Sleep murk persists, but the words cut through its fog and straight to my brain and then the gut.

They're the type of words you dread hearing. Ever. Like the sudden stomach punch after answering a phone call and being told the unexpected. Someone saying they have "bad news." Out of the blue. Day to night in a moment. The sense of falling. And nausea. You want life to remain the way it was in those seconds before answering. For time to stop.

The same with an unexpected knock and a door pushed open. The urgency precedes the words. They're not the tentative "I've got to tell you something....," but the ice cold water poured on your placid and sleeping face.

The words then. Hard slap to consciousness. Something about "an accident." Needing to go out to the track. Quickly. A broken leg. That part doesn't want to register in the brain. Numbness. Going through the motions of getting up, rapidly moving through the kitchen, heading out the door and to the back of the house. The open field spread before you. The reality shimmering with the heat. To the west, the ridge and the familiar lay of the field. To the east....unthinkable.

Then running. But not leading a horse, sulky and driver. Not far to go. No time to hold onto the seconds before the harsh reality further congeals.

Seeing them all-too-soon. They're right at the first bend in the track, near the squat, lone white pine that has grown to about thirty-five feet now. It doesn't grow during that moment. Time freezes. Wanting it to go backward, but it refuses to cooperate.

The sulky was unhitched and shoved into the field. It whispered of immobility and an empty barn smelling of old wood and memories and the photos that would be the only indication of what was once, but is no more. Photos starting to curl up in corners and the colors dulling in a yellow pallor. Almost jaundiced.

A winning horse.

Seeing him hold the reins to the horse, whose eyes screamed wide with utter confusion and fear as the one leg would slowly lower, barely touch the ground, be pulled up, its lower part dangling loose in a grotesque, unnatural way. Feeling that split-second destruction of the grace and vitality of this animal. The horse looking around for some answer and at his surroundings, which had been so familiar and friendly and now must have seemed alien and malevolent. He looked towards a sky beneath which he used to dance and pace and sweat with exuberance.

The vet there in a flash. Or taking forever. Time not feeling real.

It was all so very quick then. So very clinical. A few seconds. How all can change in a flash.

The long needle, the quick insertion, a gut-wrenching groan, the beautiful, proud beast collapsing to the ground in a heap. The thump. The expelling of gas.

The thin line of our existence was all too apparent on that awful afternoon. Running with confidence and in his complete prime. Something slightly off, out of balance. Then everything gone in an instant. Just from one, single...

....misstep.

Twenty-three acres contain many such stories beneath their soil. Sadness, happiness and joy, disappointment, anger, depressing, inspiring. So very many. This was just one more tragic one that no one else will ever know about once we're gone.

XII. Buried

I'm not sure how many horses are buried under those acres. They didn't go in the main parts of the field where plowing and planting were occurring season after season, but on the edges. I suppose if they were deep enough. Life from death.

There are also many family pet dogs and cats buried here and there. They all used to prowl and patrol and bounce through the thick grasses in the summer or deep snows in the winter. They all were, during their time and like the succession of trees, an essential ingredient of this space. They each defined a place and time in our lives.

They all left tracks like those little bird feet on that eight-by-eight square plot of land I carefully monitored in high school. I can still see them. I wonder if others, if they look or listen hard enough, might detect them as well. Or me. Something vague in the peripheral vision in the haze of a July day. Maybe a movement. Gone when you turn to look. The hint of a moan within the wind sweeping across crusted snow on a February night. A yip and howl that is probably just a coyote.

Probably.

Listening intently but then not hearing it anymore.

XIII. Expectations

There is a lot of predictability in a piece of land. At least during your time with it. At least some of the time. Or, at least, it may appear to be that way.

At times.

For instance, you know that in August, goldenrod will begin to suffuse the field with its bright yellow flowers. It's as though the plants have been soaking up the sunshine all summer long and then release it as the fall begins to creep closer and the sun slowly edges back to the south. The staghorn sumac that venture to the edges of the track will splash in brilliant orange and red before the leaves on other trees decide to make their showy transformations, but the sumac will tend to be bright even if the foliage on those other trees is a bit duller than normal. The deer will appear in the far, northwest corner of the field, having followed the path up from the swamp, and they'll graze warily at dusk on summer nights. Sometimes they'll slowly, methodically make their way further across the field with their large ears continually turning in all directions to detect the slightest sounds that could signal danger. Closer and closer they get to the barn and the house.

A piece of land teaches about the seasons, the flora and fauna, about forest and field succession, people's impact on the environment, the weather, the geology of the landscape, your spirituality. Even within its parameters of seeming orderliness, there is nothing completely predictable or set in stone or duplicated 100% of the time each year. The blue (or cow) vetch may grow in profusion every summer in about the same areas and may appear similar as a whole, but the scene is never exactly the same.

Yes, it's a good environment for cow vetch at this point in time. But this was certainly not so 20,000 years ago when the spot was crushed under thousands of feet of creeping glacier. Or 12,000 years in the past when it was collecting sediment at the bottom of a huge body of water that has been called Lake Hitchcock and stretched from the middle of present-day Connecticut to the Northeast Kingdom of Vermont. Or even 400 years ago when it was thick forest land and cow vetch hadn't been introduced to North America yet. No, I'm afraid it's not a native plant.

There are plants that are less common, but that do exist on our acreage. I'm thinking, in particular, of some wild asparagus that have grown each and every year in the same three spots. I'm not sure the first time my mother mentioned seeing them. I think it was back when I was in college in the late 1970's or so. She pointed them out during one of our walks around the track and informed me that she'd been told they were edible if harvested early enough. At that time, it was too late to cut, cook and eat them. The young shoots are tender but when full-grown, are too tough to chew. She said we'd have to remember to watch for them the next year so we'd be in time to pick and try them out.

The next year we saw them once more. Again—we were too late to harvest them.

One year, Mom decided to mark them with ribbons so that we'd spy them early on the following year. Not sure what happened to those ribbons, but it didn't work. Maybe we just forgot to look or, perhaps, I didn't visit home at the right time to go search for them.

Those few wild asparagus became a seasonal landmark every year when I went around the track. One pair always grew on the edge of the thin row of poplars directly opposite the house on the north side of the track, right where it started to slope down to the swamp. Another, single one sprang up on the west side near some scattered pitch pines, oak and young white pines. A third appeared a few years later on the outside of the track near the barn and where a short spur of dirt road cuts through to the main, dirt road (Oxbow Road). These wild asparagus turn an intense yellow late in September.

Each year we would notice these wild asparagus when they'd reach that point of being just past edible. Each and every year we'd say "next year, we'll find them when it's early enough to eat them."

I've still never tasted wild asparagus, but I do know where to find it. Predictably.

At least at this point in time.

XIV. Carefully Watching

Back when I was 19 or 20 years-old, I really got into hiking. Along with its physical benefits and my general love of being out in nature, I developed an interest in observing and identifying the flora and fauna seen along my routes, as well as trying to understand more about the geology of the landscape. I bought books about wildflowers in New England and field guides and such. I'd set the goal of trying to identify something new on each trip and committing to memory the name of a flower or fungus or tree. This goal fell by the wayside, of course, but I did manage to learn to identify a few things. And I'm still trying to do this.

It always seemed as though the vegetation in our field in Newbury was pretty basic. Lots of dandelions and a few bluets on the drier edges in the spring, a scattering of hawkweed added in early June, the blue vetch and red clover coming into prominence in late June and early July along with bits of Queen Ann's lace and chicory, more black-eyed Susans, field bindweed, goldenrod and some yarrow in August, a handful of clumps of purple-stemmed asters that brought up the rear of the warmer season in a grand finale in September. In the shadier northeast corner, a few jewelweed would cluster in the richer soil that sharply contrasted with the sandier, well-drained earth and open northwest corner, where the goldenrod were quite content.

I'd always want to find some rare plant, insect, or anything else, on our acreage. Or at least something that I encountered infrequently, whether on our property or elsewhere. It was like looking for treasure, with as much enjoyment in the search as in the discovery.

This didn't happen too often over the years. A few times in the area under the huge white pine in the northeast corner, where I'd venture every few years to dig around for old bottles, I'd run across a lone plant with dark pinkish stems that each supported creamy white berries which had little black spots in the center. It was the kind of plant that you somehow knew, instinctively, must be poisonous. It was attractive, but in an ominous way. It was called a "baneberry" and I was able to remember the name by thinking of it as a potential "bane" to your life because it was poisonous.

Less intimidating and quite edible were the tangled vines of Concord grape that appeared at some point in the late 1990's. Or at least I think it was then. I was in the midst of my 17 years living on the West Coast at that time and only had intermittent glimpses of our property. Most of the trips back for visits were in August or September, though a few were in November or December.

But the grapes. They draped themselves over sumac and young red maples in that same northeast corner where'd I'd found the baneberry and beyond which, on the slope, were my bottle-digging spots.

Maybe this was a special, magical place on the property? Some convergence point? An intersection of different environments that was shaken up every few years with changes in the land?

Come to think of it, this is also where the only moose I'd ever seen on our property appeared, ambled a bit for about 15 or 20 minutes, then disappeared into the woods back towards the swamp (I presumed). And where, on one of those "you could almost hear a pin-drop," quiet nights when I was visiting home, I heard the yips and yelps of a pack of coyotes as they tracked something from the swamp to that same corner, before heading off to the east, presumably following the arc of woods that bordered the swamp.

Then again, the only tendril of green snake I ever saw was also in this section, as I caught sight of it flash in a quick crossing from one camouflage zone to another. Brilliant in its green, it quickly blended in with the grasses and became indistinguishable from its surroundings. It made me think of Emily Dickinson's poem, "A Narrow Fellow in the Grass." And Dickinson would always make me think of Mom, who loved literature and sometimes quoted from Emily's work:

"I'm Nobody! Who are you?

Are you—Nobody—too?

Then there's a pair of us!

Don't tell! They'd advertise—you know!"

Of course, there will always be exceptions to every rule. It was actually on the west side of the property where, out running on the track on a mid-summer day, I came to a full, startled halt at the sight of a three-to-four-foot long milk snake. It was stretched out before me on the packed dirt in the middle of the track, warming itself in the early afternoon sun. It's reddish and light yellow banding make it a strikingly colorful reptile. The name is the result of a rural myth—that these snakes slither into barns at night and drink milk from the cows. Actually, they're after the rats and mice that proliferate in such structures, so farmers are quite tolerant, and even appreciative of, their presence.

As for me, the green snake had been quite large enough. The primitive, perhaps innate, shiver of alarm I felt at encountering a reptile the size of that milk snake made me give it a wide berth. I preferred the more common sightings I had of garter snakes.

I've never actually seen a milk snake around the barn, though. Then again, we didn't ever have any cows and no one milks horses.

XV. Feeding Time

I remember trudging out to our eight-by-eight plot in high school on bone-chilling winter days, when there was about a foot and a half of snow on the ground.

We didn't much like getting out of the classroom at those times.

On the other hand, I can recall many winter nights when I would gladly escape homework (okay...perhaps I was lying on my bed and listening to a Yes or Pink Floyd album), pull on my boots, heavy jacket and wool mittens, and quietly sneak out the mud room door.

I guess I shouldn't assume that everyone knows what a "mud room" is, unless you're from "the North Country." Simply speaking it's the entrance area where you should "take off your muddy boots and leave them behind before you tramp into the kitchen. I mean..... Jezum Crow!" Especially during Vermont's mud season—that period of the great meltdown between winter and spring. You know. The five months of winter and the two weeks of spring.

But back to the escape.

I especially liked crystal-clear winter nights, of course, when the temperatures dropped down to the teens, single digits, and sometimes below zero. All right—I didn't venture outdoors too much when it was below zero.

I knew it was really cold when my nostril hairs froze with each inhalation and they felt crinkly. The field would lie before me on such nights—covered with snow that appeared a light gray tint depending on the number and types of clouds in the sky and the phase of the moon, spreading over to the dark shapes and deep shadows of the forest on the borders of the track and the seemingly prostrate hills beyond. If the moon was full or nearly so, the shapes of trees were readily apparent and the tint of the snow was almost bluish. On cloudy or new moon nights, however, it was a solid blackness where not much of anything could be made out and the field and woods beyond were intimidating. It made me understand why, in the days of candlelight and fireplaces only, people would hover together in their homes and stray night sounds could make them shiver with a primal and understandable fear. In those times journeys into the darkness were only for emergencies and anticipated with dread at what might lurk in the pervasive blackness. Wolves? Ghosts? The Devil? Rocky the Flying Squirrel?

The other side of the track did seem like another world at night. Somewhat dangerous. A place where you didn't know what might be staring out at you from the woods and where cracking and snapping sounds from the darkness could simply mean a small branch giving way to the steady weight of winter snow, the wood of a tree contracting with the cold, or a coyote that had caught wind of you. Those primal instincts might kick in and scream out "you're being stalked!"

When I was in high school, I spent a lot of quiet, meditative moments on such winter nights out in the barn with the door open or on the side of the field close to the house. In those years, I would feed, water and clean the stalls of Bill's horses—never really feeling it was work, but a break, a chance to connect with the place, an opportunity to be in the moment and focused on a task. And I especially enjoyed this chore on cold, winter nights. Not to mention that I truly liked the horses.

The horses would always let me know that it was feeding time. If I'd opened the mud room door quietly, their response would be delayed, but just until my footsteps landed in the enclosed hallway leading past the woodshed, through the storage room, past the two-seater outhouse (with the sign for "Wall Drug of South Dakota" hanging over the creaky, latched door), then out through the two-car garage that adjoined the house to the barn. The horses would stomp on the floorboards of their stalls or slightly kick their hoofs against the walls to let me know that I needed to get a move on as I drew closer. I'd also hear their happy nickering in anticipation of dinner coming. Usually it would be one horse who first detected my being on the way. Then its excitement would spread like wildfire to the others.

Classical and operant conditioning, I would read, a few years later in a psychology textbook at college. After all, horses don't actually "get excited" or feel "happy." You're anthropomorphizing.

Fine. I do it all the time without apology.

There's a tangible silence and stillness on bitter, clear winter nights. It's as if the planet is holding its breath and contemplating the star-filled skies and its own place within the universe. Each and every sound seems particularly crisp and distinct. You feel very tiny, but content, in this dark expanse. Your every breath eases out slowly and dissipates. It seems that bits of your essence go with it to join with the atmosphere and the heavens.

"Let go and let God?" Or the Great Mysterious. Or who needs to define the feeling, just go with it. Or whatever.

Heading to the barn, I'd turn light switches on in succession along the way to ward off imagined night creatures and, more practically, to avoid unfortunate collisions--in the hallway next to the woodshed outside the mudroom door, in the storage room, then the garage. Finally, I'd have to enter a side section of the main barn and slide a wheeled, wooden door to the side. Its high-pitched sound would further excite the hungry and alerted horses. Dinner! "Me first, me first," I could almost hear them telling me. Then I'd navigate my way into the main part of the barn, my hands groping in the dark to find the string attached to a lightbulb that hung overhead in its center. Except on moonlit nights, this part of the barn was almost pitch black and the thumps and snorts and nickering of the horses would be comforting as the child within me, once again, whispered of hands reaching out from the shadows to grab me.

Too many horror movies and episodes of "The Outer Limits" in my childhood years, you know.

There were three stalls on the left side of the barn as you entered from this direction. To the right were three more. One was directly next to the barn's main door, and another two and a storage area were before it in a separate section to the right. I don't think there was any time in our years on the farm when Bill had horses in every one of those stalls. He usually used at least one or two to store equipment and/or hay bales.

The grain bin was in the right section as you faced the field from inside the barn. The loft above was where the 800 or so bales gathered in the summer were stored. About a week's worth were regularly dropped down to the storage area in the lower, right side of the barn for easy access. It would always be a chore to wriggle my fingers between one of the two, tight strings that kept the rectangular hay bales together and to pry one of them loose at one end. I'd attempt to loosen it a bit, then kick in the middle of the bale so that it would break open. Once that was done, of course, the released hay would erupt, escaping outward from the clutches of the other string and break up into what Bill called "leaves." These were distinct, little sections of clustered hay that held conveniently together in approximately the same amount, and each horse would get two, such "leaves" for their evening and morning feedings. Each horse also got a large can full of grain.

Every time I broke apart a bale of hay, my nostrils filled up with that aged, musty, memory of summer smell, reminiscent of green grass, bumblebees landing on various flowers, humidity settling in haze, sweat and drowsiness. I'm sure that the horses, too, had fleeting images of grazing in open fields, galloping across the pasture, crunching sweet mouthfuls of alfalfa and clover.

Oh wait, there I go "anthropomorphizing" once again. They only have instinct, after all. Stimulus and response. Right.

Part of my feeding chores included bringing plastic buckets back to the house and filling them with hot water from the kitchen faucet. This I'd use to help thaw out the water buckets that were in each horse's stall. At this point I'd need to unhitch the main barn doors and open them outward to the paddock and the field beyond.

And the night sky overhead.

Somehow, this always felt like some mystical experience. The confines of the barn with its artificial light. A pervasive silence except for the knocking of hooves and the sound of the horses crunching on hay and grain. The doors creaking open and the expanse beyond, indistinct in its land forms which I could imagine to be anywhere, unexplored, unknown, beyond the easy definitions of humanity, beyond the categorizations and the maps and the textbooks. There was the sky overhead, sprinkled with the countless pinprick lights of the stars if it was a clear night.

It was at these times, on cold winter nights, when those 23 acres melted into infinity. Everything was amplified and immediate. My boots crunching in the snow, which was packed from my previous walks to the water-filled, old claw-footed, bathtub. Exhaling my breath. The continued movements of the horses in the barn. A few miles down on Route 5, which was less than a quarter-mile east from our house, the downshifting of a tractor trailer truck. On rare occasions, the eerie howls and yips of coyotes up on the ridge to the west. They were still fairly new in returning to the "North Country" back in the 1970's. The hooting of an owl somewhere in the vicinity of the swamp.

The horses' water buckets were usually full of solid ice on such winter nights. I'd carry them outside, bang them on the ground once or twice, and much of the time the ice would loosen and come out in one chunk with a "thump" onto the snow. Other times it wouldn't be so easy, but if I poured just a bit of the hot water over the buckets, then it would eventually break the icy grip on the plastic. Next, I'd go over to the bathtub that stood on the edge of the paddock. A hose ran from the backside of our house directly into it and the water was left on by Bill so that it wouldn't entirely freeze in the cold months. I could partially refill the horses' buckets with cold water and mix it with the hot that I'd brought out from the house. This would enable the very thirsty horses to gulp long drafts of the water after having crunched down their grain and munched on the dry hay for several minutes.

The water routine always followed my pouring grain and tossing in hay for each of the horses, as they'd be occupied with eating. I'd easily be able to go in the stalls and take out the water buckets without worrying about their edging around me to escape and head out for a little amble down the road or wherever else they might want to check out.

I never once worried about the size of the horses or of their kicking or trapping me in the stalls. Maybe I should have, but I always felt comfortable around them. I'd be amazed that with their size and power, they were willing to put up with so much from humans.

After watering the horses, and before closing the barn door, I'd pause for a minute or two and just stare out over the field, the woods beyond, the ridge, the star-filled sky......or into the cloudy, murk of darkness depending on the weather. I felt, fleetingly, in touch with everything and totally content. There certainly is something to be said for "being in the moment."

It was always with a measure of reluctance that I'd let those seconds pass and head back into the barn to shut the main door, pull the string on the lightbulb and return that space to darkness. Then I'd feel my way to the inner door and slide it shut, and return indoors to tedious homework, the now obtrusive noise of the television and whatever mood my parents were in, as well as the reality of my own, wildly fluctuating emotions.

Maybe, too, I'd get back to listening to some more of "The Dark Side of the Moon."

XVI. Measurements

A couple of years ago before writing this I learned from my parents that their property was 22 acres and not 23. Or was it 21?

Whatever. I'm not editing that "23" figure from my earlier writings. In my head it's always been 23. It reminded me that for most of my life, Pluto was considered one of the nine planets. Not a measly "planetoid!" How humiliating, that downgrade. Or the nearby Mt. Moosilauke in New Hampshire had always been listed as at 4,810 feet in elevation. This has been one of my favorite hikes over the years. I figure that I've summited it at least 12 times.

Then someone, somewhere, re-measured it and dropped the official elevation down to just 4,802 feet. So I had actually gained 96 feet less in elevation during my life then I'd figured before? The hell with that.

I think when we first moved into the house in Newbury, the acreage was estimated to be 25. I'm not sure when it went down to 23, but it hardly concerned me. After all, we weren't losing any actual ground, except for that figure in our heads that denotes real estate, values, boundaries, private property, quantification, measurement......conversations with people who want to know how much land there is at your house.

"Oh....about 25 acres or so...." Sounds more impressive than 23. Or 22.

With most, who may have postage stamp-sized lawns, it doesn't really matter if it's 15 or 20 or 27 acres. To them, anything over a half-acre is huge. The very number "25" seems to evoke images of wide-open spaces like the vast farmlands of the Midwest.

So much of that figure strikes me as absurd now. In fact, the whole concept of property ownership registers as insane in my head. As the Native American people would say, how can you own the land, the water, the air? But American-style "capitalism," expansionism and the arrogance of "Manifest Destiny" have never been anything in which I believed. Thankfully.

Indeed, how can one own thoughts or emotions or time or a process? Everything on a bit of land that we try to enslave with barbed wire or blueprints is in constant flux. It's as though we're just viewing a passing stream from a set point that is only a specific spot in our limited existence, in our (so-called) logical brain, and in our desperation to affix a definition to a place and time. Hell, with plate tectonics, erosion, glacial ages and comet or meteor strikes, not to mention the planet's rotation and orbit around the sun, black holes, the Big Bang, string theory, etc. the whole idea of a truly fixed point is rather absurd.

But such thoughts can drive one....crazy? Or just make your head hurt. You still have to be up at 6:30 a.m., as rudely reminded by your alarm clock, to get ready for work, which is at a specific address, you think. It takes so many minutes to get there over so many miles, as measured on your car's odometer or indicated on your map. Oh yeah.....or told to you by your GPS. Profound thoughts only open up what seems like an abyss inside. Precise measurements and predictability, all in black and white, are so...comforting.

So....22 instead of 23 or 25 acres. Or an 8-foot by 8-foot square of land on the side of a hill for a high school biology class that maybe we measured incorrectly and was actually 8'2" by 8'11". Perhaps. I'll never know for sure. My memory, too, may be off and it actually was a 10' by 10' space. In fact, the slope itself, where that plot was located is now long-gone. It was eventually excavated to put in a playing field.

So, the change in the number of acres in my head doesn't alter the lay of the field, the slope down to the swamp, the row of gnarled, sugar maples, the tiny bird tracks indenting the newly fallen snow. At least in my lifetime.

Anyway, what truly bothered me is that the estimated date for when our house was built was changed.

XVII. Dreams

Dreams can come alive on a piece of land. They can be nurtured and grown there.

They can be maintained even when venturing far beyond that bit of earth, where realities are quick to sober you. Such dreams can be heard on crisp, January nights when the occasional crack of ice on the nearby frozen Connecticut River reverberates across the half-mile from that bend in the river called the oxbow all the way to a back porch.

Dreams whisper in your ear from years past when you closed your eyes and your feet, snug in hockey skates, pushed off from the edge of the track onto a frozen pool. It had been created by an end of January thaw with its snowmelt and heavy rain. You then glided across it towards the countless stars pulsating with the lights emitted from hundreds of thousands of years before you stood in that spot.

On how many acres? Over how many many light years? At what age?

There was that one winter in high school when the elements and the field worked just the right magic. At the time, I was obsessed with ice hockey and, though I could barely skate and was already fifteen years old, with no ice hockey team within 35 miles on which to play, I was determined to learn the game. Of course, first of all, that required becoming a good skater. Or, at least, an acceptable one.

Most years in Vermont there's a mid-winter thaw. At least that was the way it was in the old days before the ravages of climate change. The thaw usually occurred in late January or, perhaps, early February.

In 1975 we'd had a lot of snow up until the end of January. About a foot-and-a-half was on the ground at the time that a mass of warm, wet Caribbean air (warm, meaning temps in the low 40's) and rain came sweeping up the east coast and turned roadsides to slush, driveways to muck, while condensing and reducing the snow pack considerably. Massive puddles were created everywhere, with some growing to the size of small ponds. In our field, cut cornstalks that were a foot or less high began to poke through the snow in most parts.

Small pond-sized pools of water formed in several parts of our undulating field where the land dipped or was slightly depressed. One of these was just beyond the track near our house and this turned into what looked like a long, shallow, oval pond that appeared to be over a foot deep in spots. I'd guess it was at least 200-250 feet long and 50-75 feet wide in the main section.

Of course, Vermont thaws are quickly followed by the return of winter with a vengeance. Often this means the extreme of an Arctic front barreling down from Canada—perhaps the aptly named "Alberta Clipper"--and plunging the daily highs from the low 40's or mid-40's to somewhere in the teens, single digits or lower. The end result? A quick freeze of all of the standing water and the rest of the snow surface turning into an annoying crust that was always a real pain—and exhausting—when you attempted to tromp through it.

That's what happened in this winter of '74/'75, as I recall. Within a day or so, all of the little temporary ponds in our field turned to solid, smooth ice. It wasn't even roughened by any of the snow squalls that often precede the blast of air from the North Pole or if it was, they petered out before the standing water had frozen. The only place where the ice was really rough was near the edges of these temporary ponds, where the water was shallow enough so that the corn stalks were visible. After this deep freeze, the ice on this standing water transitioned slowly on the outer edges into a thinner layer and then, almost imperceptibly, into the crust that covered the remaining snowpack on the rest of the field.

Wanting to practice my skating and trying to learn to stickhandle and shoot a puck, but with the nearest skating rink 35 miles away, this development was perfect timing for me. The best part, too, was that we didn't get much more precipitation or warm weather for the next four to five weeks or so. Thus, the skating rink remained for all that time.

So, virtually every night through February and early March, I made my way out to this private, skating rink.

XVIII. Skating at Night

It's an ideal night. Temperatures in the low 20's and clear, with a waxing, gibbous moon hanging out overhead. The skates are always in the mud room in order to stay warm and flexible. Their blades are covered with leather guards that allow me to walk in them on the floor, across the cement on the back patio, and through the yard. This protects the blades and keeps them sharp.

Wool for socks, gloves and a cap. Snug in the puffy winter jacket. Jeans suffice on a warmer night—meaning at least in the teens for temperatures. Need for flexibility, but knowing that once moving about, the body heats up pretty quickly. One light pair of white socks, followed by the wool ones. The feet can't be loose in the skates. Need to be tight for maximum control. The downside—feet get cold much faster. Making sure there are no wrinkles at all that would be irritating. Pulling on the skates and lacing them up tightly.

Heading out the door and grabbing the hockey stick and the puck in the hallway next to the wood shed. Walking carefully and a bit awkwardly out to the cement back patio, stepping down onto the well-worn path in the snow and over the lawn, across the track, to the edge of the ice.

There's a certain smell to a winter night. Almost pristine. Cleansing for the nostrils and lungs. Here it hints of the flow of the nearby Connecticut River under jammed ice, hemlocks swarming on the sides of the huddled hillside and smoke billowing out chimneys from wood fires crackling in warm living rooms across the countryside. There's a stillness as if the sky is waiting for someone to venture forth, as though it's a stage before the whole universe, as if there's a baited breath that will only be released slowly as feet crunch the snow, echoing across the constellations, a trajectory straight towards release and speed and muscles pushing and in tandem with the images inside the head and dreams in the heart.

The first step onto the glistening surface. Tentative. Carefully getting a feel for the new interface, the unique relationship between legs and feet and elevation and balance of sharpened metal against ice. Not the most natural of relationships. The legs stretching, questioning and searching for the familiar, then remembering and the whole body following suit. Strides lengthening. The field stretching off to the horizon and skating full-fledged towards it. Breathing faster and pulse quickening.

Push off and glide, push off and glide. Left skate, right skate, left skate. The rhythmic sound of blades digging into the ice. Faster, faster. Then a few bumps marking the end of the natural rink and the scattered, dark spots where the cut corn stalks act like speed bumps. Eventually the ice thinning to a sheet that will crack and break under my weight. Practicing my abrupt stops right before that. Turning around and repeating this in the opposite direction.

No lights on the hillside, across the field, in the trees immediately beyond. Only a single streetlight, along the main road, about a mile distant, always just barely visible through the trees at the north end of the field. Looking back at the house, where smoke curls out of the family room chimney, the kitchen's features barely visible through the picture window. Seeing the light left on in my bedroom. The radio still tuned in to the station 160 miles away in Boston, where the Bruins play hockey and 15,000 people cheer.

Under the sky. On the ice alone. The quiet. The solitary sound of trying my best. Whatever the result.

XIX. Richard Wright

"Hold fast to dreams, for when dreams go, life is a barren field, frozen with snow."

Reading that line from a Richard Wright poem at my high school graduation, over two years later. *

The ice rink never again formed like that in the field. Never again to that degree in the nearly 40 years since. Maybe it will someday in the future. For someone else. Whether that person skates or not.

Maybe someone will read these lines. Or one of those poems I wrote that spoke of Mom exploring back roads and wanting to choose those less travelled.

Remembering when I rattled to a stop as the ice ended on the snow-covered field. Remembering when I turned around, without pausing, for a harder skate back in the opposite direction and thinking, only, of the gliding and the night sky overhead.

*Using that same line to introduce the first section of my self-published book of poetry. Forty years on. Showing it to my mother. In the nursing home. Mom. Who drove through snow-storms and shivered in the stands at my hockey games when I was 17. Who waited patiently with Bill near an overpass of Route 91, at the bottom of a long hill, where I, then age 29, was one of the hundreds of triathletes zipping by on my racing bike. Who sat in a coffee shop in Seattle a dozen years later listening as I read my own poetry before a small gathering. (**NOTE:** This paragraph was inserted 7 years after writing these essays).

XX. Family Dog

Took up running to get in shape for soccer season towards the end of each summer when I was in high school. Ran about three or four laps on the track—1.5 to 2 miles. Our dog at the time, named Muffy (or Muffet, Muff-Stuff, Wile E. Coyote, Fang and any of the other affectionate nick-names we had for her), would always enthusiastically follow me. She was just two to four years old then. Medium-sized dog with what Mom called strawberry blonde fur. A mix that was mostly collie and husky, though they said maybe a bit of German shepherd in her too. We called her a "colluskie." A beautiful and truly sweet dog. When Bill trained the horses, she'd give chase for lap after lap. Amazing energy.

In college. Was running almost every day and when visiting home would always do three to six miles on the horse track. In the summer, the swarms of deer flies would drive me to distraction. They seemed to congregate in the northwest and southwest corners of the property, where it was drier. Don't know why. Seemed to like the area around some pitch pines too. They like dry, sandy soils.

"Go for a run," were words that Muffy knew all too well. She'd get excited and whimper and bark before I opened the mudroom door. Knew we were headed out to the track. She'd trot along for the entire way on my runs, sometimes taking a break near the house to get a drink of water at the bathtub outside of the barn, but then b-line back to me as I neared the first bend. Occasionally she'd be sidetracked by a chattering squirrel or something unseen rustling in the brush. She'd disappear for a minute or two, then usually reappear ahead of me or charge up from behind.

She also knew the words "go for a hike." Didn't go out the back in the direction of the track, but to my car when I said them. Was my companion on dozens of day hikes and some back-packs in the White Mountains. Did Moosilauke, Lafayette, Jefferson, Kinsman and Liberty and others. Camped in Tuckerman's Ravine and in Zealand Notch. And many more places.

A few years later.

Watching from the picture window as Bill trained a horse and Muffy followed for a lap or two. Then, around the third lap, she backed off and cut a diagonal charge across the field to intercept him on the far, northwest corner. Then she'd finish that lap, trot over to the bathtub in the paddock, sip some water and head to the mudroom door or the front yard to lie down.

Graduate school. "Go for a run," excitement and whimpers and yips. One or two laps, then the pause for a drink. Urging her back out on the track and her walking to the garage and looking back. Teasing her with a "don't be a lazy dog!" Maybe coming back out later for another lap. Or just a few hundred yards. Maybe lying down on the grass and just watching, her tongue hanging out.

Not knowing, at that point, what was probably going on inside of her. And the likely pain she was in.

Several jobs. Many disappointments. The runs when I visit the farm now on roads into the village and up into the back hills. Lots of variation in routes and different sights. Doing the trail on the ridge or a dirt road loop through forest and by farms. Spotting deer, a coyote, a weasel bounding across the road after a mouse, forget-me-nots growing along the stream on the road heading a mile uphill towards the lake. Picking up the pace on occasion with a new dream of spotting the finish line in the half-Marathons or triathlons for which I was training.

Later. A cool-down of going one lap around the track. Old time's sake.

Pausing at the first bend in the east. Slumping fence posts and tangled wire. A few young birches. The huge rock nestled in the grass. A chunk of quartz coated with the translucent bits of mica. We first found this rock in the woods behind my grandparents' house in Monson, Massachusetts when I was about six years old. Another place. Another time. It was about two feet long. We lugged this beautiful stone from one house to another every time we moved over the years. It ended up here.

It was a fitting marker for her. It won't be moving again on our account.

Damn, I loved that dog.

XXI. Eye Blinks

Standing on the back patio and looking out at the acreage.

Blink.

The end of a humid, August day. The sun dipped beneath the ridge and a watercolor mix in the sky--orange, red, pink, yellow, shades of blue. Deep smell of tilled soil and ripening corn and cut grass in the yard. The fence gone from around the paddock, the remaining fence decrepit around the vegetable garden close to the house.

Fading light and indistinct shapes. The field blurring, seeming in motion.

Blink.

There was a piece of rusted, old farm machinery amidst the new growth in the northwest corner of the property. Near the stand of tall white pines. Maybe something that turned the hay over to dry before baling? Now partially hidden by the tangled grass, amidst poison ivy and pine needles, scrub oak and clubmoss. One year it disappeared. Not sure who would want it. Not sure of to where it went. Does Bill remember or know? Have never asked.

Blink.

The few years when we had the snowmobile. Relatives and friends from Massachusetts visiting in the winter and testing it out, crisscrossing the field in random patterns. Aiming for momentum by following the curve of the track. Grindingly loud and spewing exhaust. Noisy but kind of a novelty. Part of living in the North Country. Kept in the storage space near the wood shed. During my late high school years and into college. Not sure where it eventually ended up. Sold? Everyone lost interest.

I preferred x-c skiing anyway. Much quieter.

Blink.

A hot air balloon floating in the sky one summer day. Navigating the Connecticut River valley. Nearing dusk and the sun skimming the ridgeline. The conditions to keep it aloft fading and needing a spot to land. Silently drifting down to what was a hay field at the time. The people knocking on the front door. Asking if it's okay to drive out on the track to load up the deflated balloon and the grounded basket and pick up its crew. Who would ever say no to that?

Blink.

Absolute stillness and distant rumbling. The smell of ozone, the sweet odor of grasses, clover, vetch, maple opening up to the coming rain. Late day thunderstorm sneaking up from behind the ridge in slate gray clouds and thunder that shatters the stillness. Pouncing with a rush of wind that shakes leaves. Turning up the pale bottoms of the poplars, all yin-yang waving with this change of mood. A lone deer staring from the open field back to the adjoining woods.

The storm passing a mile or so north, as usual, the winds bending the trees at the opposite

side of the track, the rain cutting through in quick sheets, the humidity relieved for a time, the heat forced out in a heavy breath and a fog hovering across the field as dusk advances. Puddles on the track sprinkled with the curry powder-colored pollen blown from white pines. Muddy brown water coated with its yellow. Drowsy insects encouraging the darkness forth.

Blink.

Mud season. The first day when spring teases and the temperatures rise towards 60 degrees and the scattered sheets of hard-packed snow and ice slowly melt into slushy puddles and retreat into the shade of the woods for last stands. The squish of the mud under boots and the smell of water newly transformed from solid to liquid. The first red-winged blackbirds debating and rambling and excited somewhere in the canopy of trees down in the swamp and a lone hawk tracing circles beyond, above the ridge. A crow caw-cawing and flapping away from a white pine.

Blink.

Orange and pink vying for the sky above Black Mountain and Mt. Moosilauke. The leaves newly unfurled, light in shade, eager to sip from a sun edging higher up in the sky.

A cacophony of sound. Seeming chaotic while at the same time perfectly ordered. Each occupying a niche. Each to which the ear can latch on and flow with the songs over the field and continue to the horizon. The "here sweetie" of the chickadee. The insistent "birdie, birdie, birdie" of the cardinal. The robin, that found its worms early in the day, serenading the sun.

The birds singing spring into the landscape. Each with their distinct and perfect tones.

Blink.

The brilliant foliage on the hillside mostly muted, settled into browns and relative dullness. Subtle shades, tones and beauty to a discerning eye. A previous night's wind left the poplars with a diminishing cover of yellow. The field opened up again, the grasses no longer vibrant, the yellow mostly drained from black-eyed Susans, the asters' purple disappeared weeks ago as if having flown south with the geese. Broken remains of cornstalks and exposed soil littered with scraggly husks and kernel debris. Dozens of crows perched on oaks, another group on a small pitch pine, many more already prancing about and pecking at the bounty left on the ground.

Blink.

Late summer day. A haze hanging over the field and bordering woods. A drowsy, early evening. Rounding the last bend on the track after a walk, and the movement of the bird in the tall grass. The wing that hangs as if broken, the unsteady gait. Getting too close and the bird shooting off with a high-pitched "deee-deeee-deeee-deee!"

A killdeer. Easy name to remember, but kind of odd for a field bird acting as a decoy to protect its chicks. "Kill a deer" a strange pneumonic.

Blink.

No clicks. A reel, but more real than that. Just a brook trickling by. The stream in back of our old house. The stream that once flowed from the edge of a glacier. The river that curved, encountered rock, cut a new channel, left behind swamp and piles of rich soil where corn, grass or pumpkins could grow.

A lake forming. An island. A continent rising. A mountain worn to the root. A river cutting through again.

One day. The reel continues. Blurs.

Blink.

XXII. Manure Pile

The horse manure pile grew throughout the year. When I cleaned the horse stalls during my high school years, I'd pile the poop and urine-drenched sawdust in a wheelbarrow and take it straight into the field, directly across the track from the barn.

On frigid, winter mornings, I'd look out the kitchen's picture window and see enormous clouds of steam rising up from this mound of horse manure. It made me think: why can't the heat from this be harnessed?

Many years later I thought about this again and read of houses in Scandinavia which would keep farm animals underneath for the purpose of taking advantage of this heat. This has been done for centuries.

Not exactly what I had in mind. Then again, I've never been an entrepreneur.

XXIII. Winter

"Hold fast to dreams, for when dreams go, life is a barren field, frozen with snow."

Richard Wright again. Funny how his lines have come to me throughout my life.

That 8′ by 8′ plot near the high school was frozen that winter, but as we learned—or I think we did—it was hardly barren.

The same with our 23 acres. Or 22 acres.

You've got to come to terms with the winter if you live in Vermont. Most years, the season lasts at least a solid four months, with little (occasionally big) hints of it thrown in during November (or earlier) and it usually ends up feeling like company after too many days—overstaying its welcome well into April.

Maybe not smelling like old fish, though.

The reality is that some winters last fully half the year. At least they sometimes did before climate change made it all so much more unpredictable. Not that the weather in Vermont is ever predictable.

So, getting outdoors on a regular basis is therapy for avoiding cabin fever, as well as couch potato-itis and the resulting excess poundage. Especially, in terms of the latter, if you have a mother who is an incredible baker and overall great cook. Poppy seed cookies that no one else can duplicate. The apple pie technique learned from her mother with its crust to die for.

Most Vermonters enjoy the snow in various ways, from downhill and cross-country skiing, to snowshoeing, ice skating, snowboarding, ice fishing and snowmobiling. Or building snow forts and sledding if you're a kid. Then again, just a daily walk in the brisk, biting air can serve to keep you sane and healthier, as well as gain an appreciation for everything that lies within, beneath, above and around those....

"....barren fields frozen with snow."

Don't pay attention to that man behind the curtain saying how much he hates the winters. And all of the natives who tell me that no, Vermonters most assuredly don't enjoy the snow.

It was always convenient that Bill used to get the track plowed in the winter back when he had horses. This enabled him to continue training them year-round. It also meant I could do runs or walks out on the property without having to deal with snowshoes or x-c skis if I so chose. And even on those Alberta Clipper days, when the wind was whipping clouds of powder off the snowpack and a few layers of insulation were barely enough to deter the penetrating cold, a walk around the track was always full of pleasant surprises. When the landscape is pared down to its bare essentials in the winter months, you learn to notice so much more.

Animal tracks.

I'd bought a book about identifying them in the winter, but never remembered to bring it with me. Usually it was too cold to take my hands out of my gloves and hold onto it anyway. Oh sure, I'd say "I'll remember what that track looks like and then look it up in the book when I get back indoors," but after warming myself, taking off the layers and boots, and then grabbing some hot coffee, I'd somehow forget. Or I'd realize that some tracks resemble others too much. Often the differences are very subtle or difficult to discern in the snow.

Still, deer tracks are pretty easy to spot. And those of little critters like squirrels. Bird tracks are obvious, though I couldn't tell them apart unless they were big crow marks. Little grooves indicated something small venturing across the snow's surface and tempting hawks or owls at night. On occasions, a tuft of fur, some feathers or drops of frozen blood would tell of conflict and prey being caught. Often, the patterns of tracks would read like a story. Sometimes that story was pretty unconventional and abstract and I'd look for another book. But I'd still look.

Plants.

No, they aren't vibrant and lush and green in the winter. Or flowering in a variety of colors. Nor are they carpeting the landscape and attracting bees, birds and insects. Well, maybe a few birds in the winter. They don't smell of much of anything either.

Everything is reduced to the basics in winter. It's mostly about shapes and textures, though some color remains in muted, subtle shades. One thinks of skeletons, foundations, frames. Much lies underneath the snowpack, of course, but even when it is deep, milkweed stalks still reach up, with the grayish, empty vessels of their pods hanging near the tops, the silken milkweed long ago having floated away on autumn winds.

The gray-brown stalks of black-eyed Susans also cluster in spots, topped off with the dark brownish, round centers that had been adorned with yellow petals in the summer. If the snow is not deep, one can also pick rabbit's foot clover and other plants that make for interesting seasonal bouquets that focus on form rather than color.

Hidden.

When we first lived on the farm and I took my dog, Muffy, out in the winter to walk the track, I was always amused by what I thought was an odd behavior of hers. She would suddenly perk up her ears, strike a statuesque pose of intense attentiveness, then do this little pouncing move that resembled a deer bounding through the woods. I thought it was hilarious. Of course, I later learned that coyotes and wolves do the same thing because they're actually hearing all of the little critters that live under, and scurry about, beneath the snowpack. And those little creatures are meals for them.

There's this open area that can develop under the deep snow and above the ground called the subnivean zone and it's a whole other world in the winter months. Insulated, it's an active living space with mice, voles and shrews and maintains a tolerable climate, with temperatures just a bit below freezing, compared to the usually frigid, windy conditions reigning on the top of the snowpack. Those critters also will venture into the upper levels of the snow and that's when they are most in danger from predators such as coyotes or owls. However, smaller enemies such as vicious weasels can, and do, wriggle their way into the subnivean tunnels and chambers in search of easy meals.

So that cute pounce is actually the move of a predator seeking a little snack.

Color.

I'd been living on the west coast for 13 years. Usually I visited back home in the late summer or early fall, savoring the chances to go hiking in the Green or White Mountains, swimming in nearby lakes, or catching the incomparable foliage display of the autumn. One year I paid a surprise visit during the holidays and there was a good snowpack already—about a foot and a half on the ground. I went for a walk around the track on a brilliant, blue-sky day with the temperatures in the low 20's and little wind.

Distance and time create a new appreciation for a place that you once knew so well. Everything is so familiar, but has changed as well. Is it maturity, the process of looking at the world with different eyes? It reminded me of when I was less than five years-old and we'd moved to Massachusetts from Georgia after my parents (New England natives) had divorced. I distinctly remember all of the wonders of my first spring there and the progression of nature through that season and into the summer. It was all so new and amazing.

So with this annual return to Vermont as an adult, I was surprised at the little things I'd forgotten about the region where I'd spent over thirty years of my life. I'd felt I was aware of every little nuance, every barely noticeable change in the place, but much now seemed new again, or renewed in my perceptions.

The colors on the walk around the track were the typical somber grays and browns contrasted with a snow white that was almost blinding under an unobstructed, mid-day sun. I was focused, as I remember being when I lived there, on the shapes and textures of things: the grooves and fissures and odd shapes in the trunk of an old sugar maple, the smooth, greenish-light gray bark of the poplars, the pods of the milkweeds that resembled little boats for some elfin race. Familiar, too, were the brush-like needles and muted greens of the conifers that rubbed shoulders with the deep blue sky and contrasted with the more stark-appearing, bare hardwoods. The drained shading and the overall shapes and the patterns of veins stood out on the many brown leaves that still clung tenaciously to the oaks and beeches.

I was resigned to the thought that the warmer end of the color spectrum always drifted south with the migratory birds or browned, became brittle, and then dropped to the ground to eventually transform to musty leaf litter. So I was amazed at the little, brilliant contrasts of red, yellow, orange and purple that were highlighted on the landscape. These were in the forms of the berries clustered in the horns of staghorn sumacs, which were somewhat burgundy in shade, the bright, little round red berries on winterberry bushes, the three wild asparagus that retained the yellow of their fall transition and stood upright and alone in the spots where undergrowth had crowded them in the summer, the violet of briar bushes that were only noticed as areas to avoid in the tangled, colorful foliage of the warmer months.

So many stalks and stems were highlighted as reddish tendrils in the sun, looking like tufts of hair from a distance. There were many more contrasts of color and shade than I remembered from the past in the Vermont winter landscape.

Maybe this was the result of my years spent in the Pacific Northwest and in Humboldt County on the Northern California coast--areas where the seasons were not so dramatic and extreme. There, I grew very aware of the subtleties of each season. Those little variations were less noticeable at first, after decades living in New England, where there is much drama in fall color, temperature changes, the turning of landscape from bare and brown before a winter storm, to all covered in white.

Living in Vermont years ago, the colder months were my least favorite ones because the drama was gone. Except, of course, for the fury of storms.

Now I can appreciate this time of year even more.

XXIV. Making Do

Making do. Resourceful. Thrifty.

Always considered laudable assets. Very much typical of Vermonters. Scraping a living out of the rocky hillsides.

Also a trait drilled into my parents' generation. They grew up with parents (my grandparents) that lived through the Depression and World War II years. They witnessed, and learned of, the necessary adaptations to often being short of money or the goods that it can buy. "You need to eat your dinner. Remember, there are children starving in Europe." That saying persisted into the days when I was a child in the 1960's.

We had a huge lawn around the farm house in Newbury. Maybe an acre or so. It seemed especially huge to someone who had to cut the grass, anyway. At one point our riding lawn mower, which we'd inherited from my maternal grandparents, died. So Bill bought a cheap, gas-powered, push mower.

It typically took me about four hours to cut the entire lawn. In my head I would divide it into parts just to make the task seem to go faster and to feel a little sense of accomplishment after completing each one. There were four sections and after completing two, I'd feel worthy of taking a break for a long, cold drink and maybe a snack.

At some point, the used, push lawn mower died and for much of one summer, Bill decided that we could make do with the heavy, manual one that we'd also gotten from my grandparents a few years back after both had passed. This probably added a good hour-plus to the task of cutting the lawn, as well as more of a workout for my back, shoulders and arms. At least my ears weren't ringing afterwards from the loud sound of a motorized lawn mower!

I didn't know of anyone else, at that time, who still used such a manual lawnmower. The thing was damned heavy to push too, especially over the sections of our lawn that undulated. Usually we didn't attempt to complete the whole lawn in one day.

I used to play songs in my head to make the work go faster in those days long before I-pods or even headsets. One of them was "Lawnmower," which was a song by the English progressive rock group, Genesis and which was on their album "Selling England by the Pound." In the group's early years, the lead singer was Peter Gabriel who later made it big as a solo artist. The album cover showed a worker sleeping on a bench and one of those old, manual mowers parked near him.

"Me, I'm just a lawn mower. You can tell me by the way that I walk."

So the point here. Making do, especially when the finances are lean. Within reason, anyway. Sometimes, of course, the positives may not quite outweigh the negatives.

Returning now to the back 22 acres that may someday become 23 again....

Soon after Bill had retired and decided he was getting too old to take care of the horses or to race anymore, he found that he needed something to keep him occupied and to bring in a little extra cash. So he decided to grow and sell some vegetables.

Not your little backyard garden, mind you, although the section closest to the house contained several rows of tomatoes, cucumbers, green peppers, broccoli, onions, cauliflower, summer squash, green beans, acorn squash and zucchini squash. He decided to plant about ten acres or so of the main part of the field, inside the track, with corn and pumpkins. He would, over the next eight years or so, sell huge amounts of corn and some other vegetables from his rusty, somewhat dilapidated pick-up by the side of Route 5 in Bradford, and smaller amounts which he left at the general store in Newbury. Many pumpkins were sold in-bulk to others who resold them, such as school groups who used them for fundraisers. Other people just came out back and picked their own.

Anyway, resourcefulness.

Rain is rarely an issue during the summer months in Vermont. At least that seemed to be true up until recent history, when climate change has been wreaking havoc in various ways and there have been several summers with moderate drought conditions. Watering crops on areas of large acreage has rarely required any sprinkling systems.

When large amounts of water are required for a business and you're hooked up to town water, it can be a very expensive proposition. Especially for a "hobby" or small, extra-cash farmer. What to do when there have been increasing dry spells that can, potentially, wipe out a few acres of corn and you can't afford to pay for so much water?

One August when I visited home from the west coast, the previous three weeks or so there'd not been a drop of rain. Nice for visitors looking to get in some hikes or boating on lakes, but not good for gardens. Getting up that first morning back home and having my morning coffee, I didn't see Bill and asked Mom where he'd gone. I scanned the field and track for him, paying close attention to the little rise in the field where his figure might be visible above the now-tall stalks of corn. She told me that he was down in the swamp and why he'd gone there. After breakfast, I went around the track to check out his new project.

There's that little path that leads from the track to the swamp at one point. It lies between the area where the grove of tall white pines once stood and where a cluster of young, white pines is still growing. It cuts a perpendicular route down the slope to the swamp. It looks as though a short dirt road had once been there, though its dead-end purpose is not clear. As long as my parents have lived on the farm, this has also served as a deer path and we'd frequently see deer gathered at that corner of the field—usually at dusk.

When I was in high school, this was the path I took with my dog, Muffy, to do a longer walk beyond our property. When I started running, it was also a brief alternative to the multiple loops around the track. We'd cut down this way to access the railroad tracks and run along them for a mile or so before turning back.

The spring and fall were the ideal times to go. During late April through May, wildflowers would bloom along the path: little tufts of bluets, a few white and purple violets, some bloodroot by the swamp. Clumps of bright yellow marsh marigolds would brighten the quagmire in the spring as well before the trees completely leafed out and shrouded it in shadows.

On the left side, hemlocks shaded the path, but eventually crowded the bank until a point where it was constricted down to nothing. Here, where the steep ground dipped straight into muck, there was about twenty feet of scrambling over slippery ferns and pine needles to avoid the mud that sucked at and caught boots or running shoes. Then there was nothing but a vague deer path leading to the wire fence that ran along the railroad tracks and passed by our property, forming its western boundary. Right where a gap in the fence allowed me to slip through, the ground between the woods and the rocky bed of the tracks was covered with horse tail. On several occasions I'd encountered garter snakes there.

In the summertime, I tended to avoid this path because of the notorious black fly season in June, followed by the ravages of deer flies and mosquitoes for the rest of the summer. And then the increasing undergrowth added to the difficulties of getting through.

Another tangent. It's easy to do when speaking about a place. As my mother's good friend, Marion, always used to say to Mom:

"Get to the point, Beverly!"

Back to Bill's innovation. So, on this visit home and trek out to the swamp path I noticed rubber tubing running along the track's east and north sides. It was lying a few feet off in the grass, goldenrod and other growth and it led to a sprinkler that was placed on the little knoll (actually a small rise) on the eastern side of the field closer to our house. I followed the tubing along the track and saw that it cut off down the path that led to the swamp. Continuing on, I discovered Bill mucking about along the edge of a deep, dark pool of swamp water. He had rigged a gas-powered, portable pump there and was drawing water from it into the tubing leading out to where it could be sprinkled over the cornfield. His adopted Brittany spaniel, Buck, was joyfully splashing around in a dark, duckweed-coated pool of water despite my stepfather's admonishments.

This system worked quite well for several growing seasons before it was abandoned a couple of years before Bill's bout with cancer, when my partner and I decided that we needed to move back to Vermont. During that same period my mother's mobility grew increasingly reduced due to knee and hip issues that gradually led to full joint replacements. From that point onward, working in the field became someone else's responsibility once again.

Most of that tubing still lies along the track and is now disappearing underneath grass, wildflowers, the encroaching sumac and other bushes. More clues for future residents of this land. More puzzle pieces hinting of past lives that will never be fully put together into a clear picture.

XXV. Perspectives

That balloon landing in our field way back in the early 1990's made me think: what did our property look like from the air or from a distance?

One view. Having hiked up Mt. Moosilauke in New Hampshire at least 12 times over the years, I'd often gotten a distant view of the Town of Newbury from the wide open summit of the mountain. However, it was much too far away to make out our specific property even on the clearest of days. This 4,802-footer is the southernmost peak over 4,000 feet in New Hampshire's White Mountains and its trailheads lie about 16 miles from my parents' house. However, from the top of Moosilauke, I could get a clear sense of how Newbury fit into the overall scheme in terms of the Vermont and New Hampshire landscapes. I could discern the ridge that runs beyond our property and cradles the Town of Newbury within the winding Connecticut River Valley, the cluster of small Knox Range peaks to the west (and east of Barre), the long ridge of the Green Mountains and its individual peaks such as the distinctive Camel's Hump.

A note on Moosilauke. As mentioned earlier, maps indicated it was 4,810 feet high up until recent years, when it was downgraded by 8 feet. Just as we'd had a different figure in our heads for our property's acreage. Didn't affect the views though.

Another view.

From that very ridge that can just be discerned from Moosilauke, where it courses behind the town common in Newbury, lies Mt. Pulaski. It's hardly a mountain at just over 900 or so feet above sea level (and with just less than 500 feet of prominence above the Connecticut River), but it offers a fantastic view of the Town, the river snaking through the valley beyond, with its well-known oxbow and patterned farmland, and many of the southern peaks of the Whites, all the way to the distant points of Mt. Lafayette and the North and South Peaks of Kinsman. Alas, you can just barely see our house from the lookout, but only when the trees are bare.

A better view.

Where that same ridge continues to the northwest of our house, there are several points that afford a view of our property that do put it into a whole different perspective.

When I was in high school and college, I sometimes did short hikes up on this ridge with Muffy. We usually ambled down that path at the northwest corner of our land and then followed the railroad tracks for less than a mile before cutting across a small patch of open field, then carefully negotiating through an old grove of sharp-thorned hawthorns that lay at the base of the ridge.

We usually hiked to a point just at the northern end of what my stepfather calls the "horse-shoe." The ridge, though only rising about 300 to 400 feet above the valley, is steep on the east side and it's composed mostly of very slippery, loose phyllite. That makes for a lot of scrambling to reach the top unless you walk another quarter-mile north to a spot next to Route 5 where there is a gentler slope through the woods up to the top of the ridge.

This area is full of small springs and seeps that trickle down here and there and encourage the growth of lots of slippery moss, making for uneasy footing. Hemlock, beech and birch cover the slopes, with sections of oak and pitch pine on the top where it is very well-drained, and the ground cover is broken by many rock outcrops. Deer trails meander all along the sides of the ridge and make you wonder at the incredible balance and dexterity of these creatures. Little piles of their scat mark their routes.

There are several great spots along the top of the ridge where one can sit on the exposed bedrock, which is carpeted with hardy moss and reindeer lichen, and look out at the multi-peaked hulk of Mt. Moosilauke prominent to the east of the Connecticut River, with the lower high points of Black Mountain, Sugarloaf and Blueberry Mountain vying for attention and rising upward in front of it. It's a very kinetic view. A crescendo of gradually higher points drawing eyes to the climax of Moosilauke with its rounded, bare summit.

The horseshoe itself is not dramatic, but cut into the otherwise rather even side of the ridge and with sheer drops of 15 to 20 feet and jumbled large rocks scattered below. Of course, glaciers played a role in shaping it. There is a section with very wet, spring-fed soils that supports a grove of white, paper birches. The forest floor here is adorned with ferns and colorful fungi in the summer and fall and wildflowers in the spring. It leads to the only fairly gentle slope down to the bottom of this large indentation that was cut into the ridge.

One year, for no particular reason except I'd not ventured beyond the horseshoe, I decided to do so. I soon found a spot with a panoramic view of our house and property.

It looked so small. And so completely different from this vantage point.

It's strange to live some place for so long and to perceive it a certain way. You walk it, run it, explore it, drive up to it in a car, approach it on foot from another direction, sleep on it. Years go by. Decades pass. Then you just shift your viewpoint a little bit and it all seems totally different. Both familiar and not.

The field is set in context with the expanse of the swamp and the further fields, at floodplain level, to the north. The slight elevation of the land is apparent. The White Mountains to the east grow in stature and dwarf, rather than frame or backdrop, the property.

I tried to imagine standing up here and seeing a tiny figure walking or running around the track. I tried to imagine a dark night, deep snow, the hoot of an owl, a distant lighted window with a figure standing outside in front of it and looking outward. Or someone skating back and forth on a frozen patch of mid-winter thaw on the edge of that open field.

I tried to imagine the slight movement of a barn door opening and anticipating that someone might be visible. I imagined the person in front of that barn peering into the night sky, with a full moon, and sensing something or someone standing up on the black shape of the ridge.

Looking back towards that barn.

Then I turned away.

XXVI. Beneath the Ground

The horse was sickly from the start. On his way out. Not a good acquisition.

One of those sweltering July spells, with the hills coated in haze and the air smothering, making you feel as if beneath too many blankets. Breath had actual weight in the barn. The flies buzzed in their dozens over the horseshit which sat in particularly pungent piles.

The dying horse had groaned repeatedly. An awful, prolonged process. It was in the afternoon. Bill was away. When it was all over, Mother had to call someone to bring equipment over with a pick-up.

Or was it a tractor? Hardly dignifying, but practical. The dead are not particular, after all. The horse dragged to the northeast corner, inside of the track. Yeah, it was a tractor because the hole had to be large and deep enough.

Not sure of the exact spot now. The slump in the earth where I think it was buried seems to be matched by others. The field undulates and the grass is thick here. A grove of poplars was cut, and another has shot up, with a few lost to a thunderstorm's wind shear a decade ago.

Or so. Not sure about timeframes anymore. Has it been that long?

I've no memory of where the cat is. The one that lived to be 17. The southwest corner? Where the pumpkins had been planted for six or seven years up until a couple of years ago? Or is it longer now? I had been living on the west coast for just a few years when a family friend found her shriveled form in one of the sheds months after she had disappeared. The other cat we had from that litter just vanished many years prior. Could've been caught by a fox or coyote. She was the skittish one of the two. Didn't like to be picked up. She wandered a lot. And then one day never came back.

The other dogs? Have no idea. Is it five or six dogs now? The earth holds so many secrets.

Bill liked to tell stories. And would often exaggerate. The fish that got away became the fish that he caught. And they sometimes seemed to grow in size.

But do I really know? What was exaggerated? Or if it really was?

A few years ago, while digging in the swamp where he'd developed his water pumping system, he encountered this large skull. Who knows how long it had been buried. How old is that swamp anyway? Was likely a bend in the river at one time. Soon after the last glacial age anyway. And after "Lake Hitchcock" had disappeared and only the river remained. Thousands of years ago. Okay, so maybe it could have been there at least from wooly mammoth times?

Geology is such a puzzle. No wonder I struggled to get a "B" in it in college. Okay I admit it. Was a "B-" and I was happy to get it!

Glaciers covered the landscape over a mile deep and this was 12,000 to 15,000 years ago. When they retreated, they left scattered glacial erratics (large rocks or even boulders), a chaos of rocky soil, meandering eskers, random kettle ponds, moraines where they conveyor-belted materials into huge piles.

Critters from those thousands of years ago could possibly have been here and ended up buried under the soil and muck of the swamp. The skull Bill found became a curiosity and a brief mystery. Relatives and friends couldn't identify it. Of course, eventually it only took a quick search on the internet to finally reveal it to be just a common moose. Sad. This loss of the mystery.

Digging for bottles in the usual spot last spring, I thought about all of our buried pets, the horse, the moose skull.

Or a mammoth skull. Keep the myths alive. The stories. My stories. Our stories.

Occasional bones are unearthed. Turkey dinners from a hundred years ago? Bits of colorful, broken china. Accidentally dropped? A button, a rusted coil of spring, a mutilated bucket. Outgrown clothes. Dead machinery. Giving up on the sugaring business? In need of a new plow? An argument leading to someone retreating to solitude on the edge of the woods with a bottle of whiskey, slugging it down and then tossing the empty over the bank?

Debris slides off that bank in another spot. Stuff that broke down and Bill didn't want to take to the dump. Adding to the archeological site. If bottles and cans weren't returnable in Vermont for so long, how much more might be here?

The histories, the endless puzzle pieces, the hints of people's lives.

The gully cut into the bank beyond our property line. Behind the neighbors' field. Their house built in the early 1800's or so, I think. Hundreds and hundreds of green and brown bottles. Beer and wine. Some others. Liquor bottles. Not old, though. But a clear story about someone. The man who lived there when we first moved into the farm house? Know there was hording, but that much drinking? Someone prior to him? Some other family member?

Reminded again. Not to judge based on individual puzzle pieces. We all have struggles. Don't know the whole picture.

The long winters. The roads that weren't plowed for days. The doomed marriages. The children that left and never came back. The ones that couldn't leave and should have. The regrets. Having a drink. Then another. Staring out a window towards the road to see who passed by.

The old bottles that were found ending up on a windowsill. Usually the picture window in the kitchen that frames a chunk of the 22 acres.

Maybe a niece will end up with them some day. Or they'll occupy window space in an antique shop. Or just be tossed, once again, over a bank. Some to break. Or brought to the dump.

If only they could speak.

XXVII. Walking Against the Grain

Does it really have any significance in the end? Or is it just a matter of habit, ingrained over time?

Has anyone ever really thought about it? The habit of doing that walk in the counter-clockwise direction. Or could I just be remembering incorrectly? I don't think so.

The dirt track around the 22 (23?) acres of land. It was the distance for training horses that competed on half-mile racetracks. And for people, it was just as perfect for getting in-shape with daily walks or taking visitors on a tour of the property's open expanse with its border of trees, swamp and the neighbor's field. For observing the annual changing of plantings from corn to sunflowers to a large section of pumpkins or just letting the clover, grasses and alfalfa grow up for eventual haying. It was so convenient for when I was in high school and first started running in the spring and summer to get in-shape for soccer season. I just wanted that measureable distance and the familiar anchor of our home, the horses in the paddock, the groves of trees, the distinctive sounds and smells of each season.

Yes. I do recall in later years when I was an almost daily runner and I did multiple loops around the track in order to log from 3 to 6 miles. I would, on rare occasions, switch direction once in a while. I'd go clockwise. However, it never felt....right (as it was usually, in fact, taking a left from the backyard). So when donning my running shoes and shorts and heading off the back patio and across the lawn to the track I would always start running counterclockwise.

Which is also odd, since my mother and I have always prided ourselves on taking—or at least strongly considering—the road less travelled. Hence in later years I pretty much stopped doing circles around the track when visiting home and going for a run, but chose to head out onto Newbury's back roads and even some trails such as the one up Mt. Pulaski and along its ridge. Still, I'd often feel compelled to end those long runs with a final lap around the track. Almost always going counter-clockwise.

Mom went through phases of regular walks on the familiar track over the years. And most visiting relatives and friends would take us up on offers to "take a walk around the track" and get in that half-mile of exercise while experiencing all that those 23 (then 22) acres had to offer. It was a chance to engage in casual conversation and connect with that land.

It provided perspective on our home and its place on the outer edges of the town, nestled in the wide, Connecticut River Valley, framed by Moosilauke, Black Mountain and Sugarloaf on the eastern horizon and the long ridge so close to the west, coursing north to south and keeping secret, until the last minute, the changes in weather rolling in from that direction.

Walking on the half-mile track would be an immersion in the place, in the time, in the seasons. We could be thrilled to hear the first peepers heralding the arrival of spring down in the bordering swamp. Their cacophony of peeping would begin towards sunset in April. It was a somewhat haunting sound. We'd look for ripening Concord grapes in the tangle that grew amongst the staghorn sumac in September at the second bend near the huge, white pine. We could hear a lone robin in one of the sugar maples having the last poignant, melodic word in a late spring dusk. We'd scan the dry ground for the first bluets in their modest shades near the northwest bend of the track. We'd sidetrack the massive puddles that would invariably form on the west side of the track, winter boots breaking through the brittle melting ice and sucked by the mud of those thawing times of March. We'd hurry along on January afternoons, snug in our many layers but feeling the wind sting our faces and we'd eye the picture window in the kitchen back at the house with thoughts of cups of hot tea while warming up our numbed fingers. We'd curse and wave our hands frantically at the hordes of deer flies that seemed to like the stretches of the track at the northeastern and northwestern bends. We'd see Muffy, or other dogs from later years, charging at the woodchucks that burrowed in the far corners of the field or that simply ran with joyous abandon in this vast space. We'd quicken our pace at the sound of rolling thunder from an approaching storm. We'd look in that direction for the dark gray that would mark the leading edge of one and seeing the stillness that overtook the land in anticipation. We'd feel very exposed under the skies in the open space of the field.

Mom and I would watch for those few wild asparagus that changed to golden yellow in the fall. Or note the bits of corn husk and scattering of kernels on the ground and see the deer tracks ambling down the path leading to the swamp. Mom and I might hear the killdeer take off at our approach, a decoy from a hidden nest.

A half-mile of dirt track, like the race courses where the horses would always race counter-clockwise. Remembering that was the direction that Bill and others went when out training the horses during those years, but now perplexed by many of the photos taken from those times which showed that they actually often went the other way. Or was it most often?

Clockwise.

Am I remembering something that was never true? Never was the case?

Twenty-five acres or twenty-three or twenty-two. An 8″ by 8″ plot of land or 10″ by 10.″ Clockwise or counterclockwise. Conversations and comments that you or I remember, but no one else does.

I think now, when sitting on our house's front porch, of watching the white-breasted nuthatches ambling head-first down the conifer in our yard. Their perspective is unique from all of the other birds who monopolize the heads-up view.

Time and memory. Distances and perceptions. All so fluid. And habits. Ingrained, maybe, but with a slight turn of the head...set loose?

And does it need any significance beyond being immersed in that time and place? If anyone is reading this, do they really care?

XVIII. Milestones

The milestones.

As on a long trip, where you note the first mile. The first ten. Point to the towns on the map (remember using maps?) with their assigned names and population-defined circles and get excited that you've reached one of them. Then another state line. The first hundred miles. And onward. As the miles fade into obscurity and blur in your head. As you are immersed in the journey.

Like years. Age six and going to school. Hitting teenage years, then 16 and driving, 18 and voting and graduating high school. Reaching 20 and seeing youth gone and 30 and staring at middle-age and then the decades seeming to go in a flash. It feels as though time accelerates.

Is it a year to the far bend in the track? Is it five to the top of the ridge stretching beyond? Does a decade bring you to the point where that thunderstorm brewed, the one you couldn't see until the dark gray clouds crept above the tree line to the west? How old are you when the winds rise and a downpour comes out of the sky? Are you on the other side of the track? The state? The continent? Another century?

The tent was erected where the horses once dipped their heads to nibble at scant grass, hungrily eyeing the expanse of field beyond the fence. No one needs to negotiate between the fence beams, or carefully try to step up and over them awkwardly, or make their way to the spot where the gate marks the path to the barn's entrance. There is no fence now. No gate. No one notices that one of the six-foot tables is standing where the claw-legged bathtub once filled with water from the hose that ran from the back of the house. No one knows that they are sitting and eating watermelon where I once emptied the plastic buckets of their weight of solid ice in the middle of winter while the horses stomped in their stalls.

These people likely have memory snippets of this place. Or more than fragments. Sipping coffee or tea in the kitchen and staring out the picture window. Squinting their eyes to see if any deer have appeared on the far side of the field. Pointing out the dark, black spot where a bear had begun to venture from the refuge of swamp to feast on the sunflower remains. Gathered on frigid winter days, hands in pockets, puffs of breath emitted like smoke, watching Bill pass by in a flash in the sulky with his first horse. Or his third. Remembering the names or some now escaping their memories.

These people took strolls around the track, planted vegetable gardens on the fringes, sat in lawn chairs on the back cement patio on humid, summer days as the corn ripened and filled the air with its earthy, sweet odor or followed the tractor and hay baler neatly transforming rows of second-cut grasses to tightly-wrapped rectangles to tide over the horses or a nearby farmer's cows for the coming winter.

Two children lob a badminton birdie back and forth, punctuating their activity with occasional yells. The net is spread right near the spot where a butternut tree once grew and that is now planted with flowers. A teenage couple hold hands and gaze at each other while sitting in lawn chairs set in front of the barn door. They are oblivious to all else. Dozens of people of a wide range of ages, but the majority being seniors, line up and hold paper plates that they will fill with the pork from a roast, fruit salad, corn-on-the-cob and macaroni salad.

It's my mother's 80th birthday celebration. One of those milestones. All present feel the significance, the passage of time, the whispers of their own memories and experiences, the flash of images from this particular place. And to some others, the children or grandchildren of those with such ties, it is all new and they don't know of the fallen butternut trees or collapsed fences. They run across the grass. A two year-old sits in a spot of bare dirt and is digging with fascination and unfettered wonder. They all wait anxiously for Mom's birthday cake to be cut after everyone's through with the main meal.

There are wildflowers on all of the six-foot tables. Or were they eight-footers? Black-eyed Susans and cow vetch and red clover. They were cut from the expanse of field beyond or on the edges of the track near the first bend, where the white pine continues to anchor the property and grows higher and higher. At least for now.

A four-piece band plays bluegrass and some folk music. People sing along and laugh. Later, my mother and three of her close friends, who are all members of the church choir, get up to perform one song together. All pause and listen intently as the journeys continue.

I think that I hear their voices echoing on the nearby slopes of the ridge.

XXIX. Time Slips Away

An unfamiliar pick-up is parked in the dirt road that connects the main road in front of our house to the track in the back. I can see a figure in the driver's seat. Bill is out training a horse. Circling round and round. It's about an hour before dusk on a September day.

A familiar car is parked in the dirt road that connects the main road in front of our house to the track in the back. I see two people in the front seat. They're an older couple who are good friends with my parents. They're watching Bill training a successful horse. It's about an hour before dusk on a hazy, July day. I hear a few, scattered robins in the trees bidding "good evening" with their elaborate repertoires.

A familiar pick-up is parked in the dirt road that connects the main road in front of our house to the track in the back. I can see a figure in the driver's seat. It's Bill. Mom pads carefully around the kitchen and places a heat-and-serve meal in the microwave.

She never used to buy these. She's always been a great cook.

A familiar pick-up is parked in the dirt road that connects the main road in front of our house to the track in the back. Bill sits in it for about an hour as the October sun dips over the ridge beyond the 23 acres. Or 22 acres. Boundless acres. He stares out at the track. No one is training horses there now. There are no horses in the barn. There may be some deer grazing at the far side of the field. The couple no longer appears either. They have both passed away.

Maybe an hour later, as the field darkens and the sky loses its sunset brilliance and the colors melt into deep blue, I hear the engine in the pick-up turn over and then start.

XXX. Orienting

Satellites zig-zag across the skies. They snap images of every square inch of the earth. You can turn on your computer, go on the internet, check out some place to see the lay of the land anywhere on our planet.

This Planet Earth.

Sometimes you can zoom in to a point that seems to be less than a couple thousand feet above or less. They even snap images from street level in many locations now so that you can look at a place you lived decades ago and see how it's changed. You can pan around and see the surroundings. Sometimes you can zoom in on the front door. Sometimes there's someone in the driveway that you recognize, or a car that your parents or a friend or neighbor had a few years back. You may even see your own car.

You may even see yourself.

Were you looking upward at the time?

You don't even need to visit these places anymore in this technology-laden world. You can satisfy that curiosity, that need for perspective, that craving to confirm your history and your place in your time. You can wish to have left some mark. Or you can realize that all marks wash away. Or just transform into something else. Or are always there.....in some form.

They're now talking about implants in the brain. Erasing bad memories. Or creating new ones. "Blade Runner" meets "Total Recall" meets "Universal Soldier" talks with Hal on-board the Discovery.

"Dave. I'm afraid...."

They can listen to your conversations at the kitchen table. They can check out a patch of planets a hundred light years away and speculate on life elsewhere in the vast universe. See how some of those worlds looked back when wooly mammoths roamed what is now your backyard. They will soon take a bit of preserved fur and grow another wooly mammoth. Maybe it will graze on 22 acres.

You can sip your third cup of coffee, 3,000 miles away from a patch of 22 acres, watch a chickadee alight outside the window, grab one bit of sunflower seed and fly away. You can pull up a view of 22 acres and try to guess when the picture was taken. In several spots you notice trees that you know were cut down three or four years ago. You see the track is less overgrown and more distinct than it is now. The trees are completely foliated, so it must be summer.

You don't know if you are there or 3,000 miles away or if anyone stares out the picture window or if an unidentifiable skull has yet been unearthed in the swamp. You don't know if that is your mother standing on one side of the track and contemplating, finally, cutting some of the wild asparagus that always seems to grow there and trying it out for dinner. You want to whisper in her ear to do so.

Satellites arc overhead amidst seas of stars that twinkle in the countless snow crystals frozen across a field on nights when you glide and kick through space and the boundaries only encroach when you think too much about them.

You don't think about undulations in the field around you, or what might be underneath. There is no underneath. You don't think about the edge of the frozen expanse of snowmelt as it approaches. The crusty snow. The remains of the cornstalks poking through.

You turn and skate back. You circle again and again. Until....when? And where?

XXXI. Short Story

I've written many stories—a handful published.

They may have been read by a few people or no one. Mostly no one but my mother or partner. I don't seem to care much these days.

My mother. She'd always read anything I wrote. I wish I'd written more.

One short story revolved around a disheveled, possibly mentally ill and/or homeless character in a small town. He's seen either wandering around an old house with a barn or in the nearby woods. People speculate. They are afraid of him. They don't know if he may be dangerous or not. They know nothing of his story.

There are frightening people in this world, after all. You never know. Maybe call the sheriff. Get a pit bull or Rottweiler as a guard dog to scare him off. Pull out your hunting rifle and have it handy. Just in case.

This character ends up in the barn. It's a place both familiar and not. Maybe it's part of a place he once lived or maybe it just resembles such a place. It doesn't really matter to the character which one it is. Maybe he, himself, doesn't know.

The current owners of the barn may have horses. Or they may have cows. Or they may decide to convert their house into a bed and breakfast. Or they may just tear it down and sell the weathered boards. It's now their place and time to do what they want with it. They most certainly don't want a stranger camping out in the old hayloft. Especially if the stranger could be dangerous.

Some of the old string that tied hay bales still hangs on nails on the dark, wooden walls of the barn. String can be used over and over. It can keep a broken door shut until the latch is fixed. It can hang a makeshift bird feeder from a branch.

It can be tied to stakes that mark off a tiny, eight-by-eight-foot plot of land. Maybe even 22 acres. Or 23.

You can step back from this place that has been snapshotted in your brain. You can even see it. Between eye blinks, you can always be absorbed by it.

You are always there. Somewhere. Sometime. You hear yourself saying this.

To your beloved mother as she is struggling with her last breaths.

To yourself.

XXXII. At Sunrise

There's an hour or so period just around sunrise. In the spring and early summer, it awakens the field and its surrounding environs with a cacophony of bird song. Eventually, the din breaks up into an order, as if all have been assigned their duties for the day. Then the calls become much fewer and scattered.

It's not just the robin hop and bob to the worm dance in the tilled soil. It's not only the occasional "chick-a-dee-dee-dee" tilting of a head on a maple branch. It's not just the cheerful good morning of a male cardinal to its mate in the neighbor's shady basswood.

It's the song of everything. At once. All the land, everything on it, everything within and beyond.

Listen carefully and you can hear your own name. You may even hear yourself and your own, special song. Then, just as though a switch has been turned somewhere, it all goes silent.

Or does it.....

Epilogue—February 2022

I hesitate to write this. It seems disrespectful on some level. To myself. To the spirit of what motivated me to write this series of essays nine years ago. Will it undermine the tone, the intention of what I wrote?

I have just found out that my parents' house and property of 48 years has been sold. And so much of what I wrote about, and what I dreaded over the years of eventually losing, has now come to pass. I'm trying to come to terms with it, this loss of identity, of family history, of what has been a foundation in my life, even when living 3,000 miles away for 17 years.

The house and barn and those 22 acres. Or what we thought was 23. Or 25. The space and the time.

About ten years ago my parents sold 1/3 of their land to a local farmer, as they greatly needed the money. It was the west side of the property. The few walks I took on that acreage behind the house then felt strange. Increasingly foreign. "This is actually owned by someone else," I thought as I crossed what I guessed was the approximate boundary somewhere on the oval track, over where a path once led down to the swamp and where stood the grove of white pines reaching to the sky when we first moved there. I was now walking on land owned by someone else. Then, further on, I crossed the border again. Not too far to the west of the now-empty barn.

Borders. So arbitrary. So set in our logical brains forever seeking black and white definitions. It was, after all, the same land. The same space. But no—not quite.

My dear Mom. She passed away just a year-and-a-half ago after a couple of years of failing health and residing in a nursing home. It was in the early stages of the great shut-down due to the COVID pandemic. How often have I walked around the track since then? Just two or three times, I believe. It all felt......too strange. Registering as familiar to my senses, but empty and painful to my soul. It only filled me with sadness and the realization of loss.

My stepfather, Bill, with major health issues of his own, persisted at the house and the property for as long as possible. But it overcame him too, I know. The pervasive melancholy. The sheer weight of the house, the acreage, their saturation with memories. It was time to move on for the benefit of his own health.

So in a little over a month after I write this, the house and that land will belong to someone else. In the last month I've been travelling up to it to slowly, painfully, help empty the contents of our home bit by bit. As if dismantling our history and scattering its details to the wind. Or into a dumpster, donated to a thrift store or sold by an auctioneer. Or a few pieces taken by relatives and creating other histories in different settings.

I know I have to let go as well. I have to take to heart some of the words I whispered to my mother on her last day with us. That I believed she and I were still walking around that track on a sunny, early summer day and looking for those wild asparagus that always grew in the same spots. That we're there now.

A final note on the photographs in this publication: I've searched through thousands of photos from over the years and not found a single one of the wild asparagus that grew on our property. Of course, I'd hope to find one to use in the book. I was positive that I'd taken at least a couple of them with my digital camera in the fall, when the wild asparagus turns a golden yellow that contrasts with the green grasses. Maybe that's just memory playing tricks on me. Or maybe the photo will magically be discovered at some point after publishing this. Or maybe it simply doesn't matter.

www.ingramcontent.com/pod-product-compliance
Lightning Source LLC
Chambersburg PA
CBHW041143120626
46547CB00020B/3088